For the Living of These Days

Resources for Enriching Worship

For the Living of These Days

Resources for Enriching Worship

**Edited by
C. Michael Hawn**

Smyth & Helwys Publishing, Inc.
Macon, Georgia

ISBN 1-57312-002-2 (paperback)
ISBN 1-57312-030-8 (spiral bound)

For the Living of These Days:
Resources for Enriching Worship

Edited by C. Michael Hawn

Copyright © 1995
Smyth & Helwys Publishing, Inc.®
6316 Peake Road
Macon, Georgia 31210-3960
1-800-568-1248

The paper used in this publication meets the minimum
requirements of American Standard for Information
Sciences—Permanence of paper for Printed Library Materials,
ANSI Z39.48–1984.

Library of Congress Cataloging-in-Publication Data

For the living of these days : resources for enriching worship /
  edited by C. Michael Hawn.
    iv + 106 pp.   6 x 9" (15 x 23 cm.)
    1 close score.
    May be used as a supplement to the Baptist hymnal, 1991.
    Includes index.
    ISBN 1-57312-002-2
    1. Baptists—United States—Hymns. 2. Service books (Music)—Baptists.
3. Hymns, English—United States.   I. Hawn, C. Michael.
M2122.F67 1995
                                                                94-41120
                                                                CIP
                                                                M

Cover design by Stephen Hefner

Preface

Faith is spoken, but it is also sung. Prayers are whispered in a single heart, but also voiced by a community. Faith is as old as untold generations but as fresh as each new day. As God's people, we speak universal truths in our particular language. And week after week, as we come together for worship, we seek to weave these many threads into a single cloth, varied in color and texture and yet one.

In this worship supplement, you will find many kinds of resources for worship. Here are hymns that sing of faith in new ways and hymns that address contemporary issues and concerns. Here are litanies and prayers for special occasions in the church's life: times of celebration, times of dedication, times of remembering. Here is an inclusive collection of resources, inclusive of male and female, varying ethnic traditions, and the great diversity of our Baptist heritage.

The compilers of *For the Living of These Days* celebrate the sesqui-centennial of those brave Baptists who met in 1845 in Providence, Rhode Island, following the final Triennial Convention of 1844. During this meeting, one last attempt was made to hold together the three principal Baptist missionary and publications societies that unified Baptists in the North and South. The efforts of those gathering in 1845 failed, and Baptists split. The Spirit that drove these Baptists to seek unity in the face of the powerful forces of disunity before the Civil War is still alive in many who call themselves Baptist 150 years later. This hymnal and worship supplement is an attempt to tie together many of the strands of Baptist heritage. To this end, hymns, litanies, and prayers old and new have been collected from Baptists representing not only the North and South within the United States, but also Baptist groups beyond our borders. Contributors include clergy and laity from the Alliance of Baptists (a group formed in 1987 primarily by moderate Southern Baptists); American Baptist Churches in the U.S.A.; National Baptist Convention, U.S.A., Inc.; Progressive National Baptist Convention, Inc.; and Southern Baptist Convention; as well as British Baptists; Canadian Baptists; and Baptists in Bolivia, Brazil, Kenya, Indonesia, South Africa. As Harry Emerson Fosdick, from whose famous hymn "God of grace and God of glory" comes the title of this book, reminds us:

> The church of the future can never be one of those unanimous
> sects, but rather a comprehensive communion, including in its
> fellowship, around the organizing center of a common devotion
> and a common purpose, the greatest possible variety of
> temperament and diversity of mind.   Harry Emerson Fosdick (1926)

Faith is spoken but also sung. In churches large and small. In worship formal and informal. With language both familiar and new. We offer these words and music as a resource for the expression of that faith in worship to the glory of God. Committee Task Force: (*Materials selection committee)

James Abbington	*Peggy Haymes (Literary Consultant)
Paula Clayton Dempsey	Ron Jackson
*Fred Grissom	John Roberts
*C. Michael Hawn (General Editor)	D'Walla Simmons

Special thanks to the following: James Abbington, Progressive National Baptist Convention, Minister of Music, Hartford Baptist Church, Detroit, Michigan, for consultation in the area of African-American materials; Alliance of Baptists for providing the liturgical ferment, moral support, and financial assistance to see this project through; Roger Crook, Retired Professor of Religion and Chair of Department of Philosophy and Religion, Meredith College, Raleigh, North Carolina, for researching the Index of Scriptural References and Allusions; Joyce Marie Davis, Director of the Lucie E. Campbell Church Music Workshop, National Baptist Convention, U.S.A., Inc., Denver, Colorado, for consultation in the selection of African-American materials; Carol Giesbrecht, editor of *The Hymnal* (1973) for the Baptist Federation of Canada for consultation in the selection of materials by Canadian Baptists; Treece and Kirsten Efird, who provided the computer and artistic expertise necessary to produce this volume; Perkins School of Theology, Southern Methodist University, for granting the editor a Scholarly Outreach Award in 1994, making it possible to complete this project; Paul A. Richardson, President of the Hymn Society in the United States and Canada and Professor of Church Music, Southern Baptist Theological Seminary, Louisville, Kentucky, for historical hymns by Baptists and general consultation; Smyth & Helwys Publishing, including Scott Nash, Editor-In-Chief, for the vision to publish this project, and Nancy Hollomon, for patience in pursuing the many details of publication; Mary Lou Reynolds for donating her services as a proofreader; Steven Taranto, student and friend, for his work as a proofreader for both text and music; Dwayne and Kathy Toole, Ministers of Music, University Baptist Church, College Park, Maryland, for proofreading and editorial consultation.

Cantate Domino,
Michael Hawn
Dallas, Texas
January 1995

Contents

God of grace and God of glory

Harry Emerson Fosdick 1930

CWM RHONDDA
87.87.87.7

1. God of grace and God of glo - ry, on Thy peo - ple
2. Lo! the hosts of e - vil 'round us scorn Thy Christ, as -
3. Cure thy chil - dren's war - ring mad - ness; bend our pride to
4. Set our feet on loft - y pla - ces; gird our lives that
5. Save us from weak res - ig - na - tion to the e - vils

pour Thy power; crown Thine an - cient chur - ch's sto - ry; bring her bud to
sail His ways! From the fears that long have bound us, free our hearts to
thy con - trol; shame our wan - ton, self - ish glad - ness, rich in things and
they may be ar - mored with all Christ - like gra - ces in the quest for
we de - plore; let the search for Thy sal - va - tion be our glo - ry

glo - rious flower. Grant us wis - dom, grant us cour - age,
faith and praise. Grant us wis - dom, grant us cour - age,
poor in soul. Grant us wis - dom, grant us cour - age,
li - ber - ty. Grant us wis - dom, grant us cour - age,
ev - er - more. Grant us wis - dom, grant us cour - age,

for the fac - ing of this hour, for the fac - ing of this hour.
for the liv - ing of these days, for the liv - ing of these days.
lest we miss Thy king - dom's goal, lest we miss Thy king - dom's goal.
as we seek to set all free, as we seek to set all free.
serv - ing Thee whom we a - dore, serv - ing Thee whom we a - dore.

Used by permission of Elinor Fosdick Downs

John Hughes

For all the love

L.J. Edgerton Smith

c. 1925

SINE NOMINE
10.10.10.4

1. For all the love that from our ear - liest days has glad - dened life and guard - ed all our ways, we bring you, Lord, our song of grate - ful praise:
2. For all the truth from wis - dom's light - ed page, un - dimmed and pure, that shines from age to age, God's ho - ly Word, our price - less her - i - tage:
3. For all the joy that child - hood's days have brought, for health - ful lives and pu - ri - ty of thought, God's life's deep mean - ing to our spir - its taught:
4. For all the hope that sheds its glo - rious ray a - long the dark and un - known fu - ture way, and lights the path to God's e - ter - nal day,
5. For Christ our Lord, our Sa - vior and our friend, u - pon whose love and truth our souls de - pend, our hope, our strength, our joy that knows no end:

Ralph Vaughan Williams

Al - - le - lu - ia! Al - le - lu - ia!

Call to worship 3

Eternal God, the Light that does not fail,
  we worship you.

We seek you
  not because by our seeking we can find you,
  but because long since, you have sought us.

We do not seek the sun
  but open ourselves to its light and warmth when it arises.

We do not seek the fresh air of heaven,
  but open our windows,
    and lo, it blows through.
So may our hearts be responsive to your coming
  and receptive to your presence. Amen.

Harry Emerson Fosdick

From *Harry Emerson Fosdick: Preacher, Pastor, Prophet* by Robert Moats Miller (New York: Oxford University Press, 198*'
by permission.

4
In unity we lift our song

Ken Medema

1985

EIN' FESTE BURG
87.87.66.667

1. In u - ni - ty we lift our song of grate-ful a - dor - a - tion, for
2. For sto - ries told and told a - gain to eve - ry gen - er - a - tion, to
3. For sa - cred scrip-tures hand - ed down, a bless-ed trust and trea - sure, which
4. For God our way, our bread, our rest, of all these gifts the Giv - er. Our

bro - thers brave and sis - ters strong. What cause for cel - e - bra - tion. For
give us strength in times of pain, to give us con - so - la - tion. Our
give us hope when hope is gone and make us weep with plea - sure. And
strength, our guide, our nur - t'ring breast whose hand will yet de - li - ver. Who

those whose faith - ful - ness has kept us through dis - tress, who've shared with us our
spir - its to re - vive to keep our dreams a - live, when we are far from
when our eyes grow blind and death is close be - hind, we shall re - cite them
keeps us till the day when night shall pass a - way, when hate and fear are

plight, who've held us in the night, the bless - ed con - gre - ga - tion.
home and e - vil sea - sons come; how firm is our foun - da - tion.
still whose words our hearts can fill with hope be - yond all mea - sure.
gone and all our work is done, and we shall sing for - ev - er.

Church Music/Ken Medema 1994

Martin Luther

Beloved God

Patricia V. Long

1989

PULLEN
10.10.10.10

1. Be - lov - ed God, our Fa - ther, Mo - ther, Friend,
2. Kin - dle our awe for all Thy works of grace:
3. Teach us our frag - ile is - land home to share
4. Help us to cher - ish eve - ry child of Thine,

source of our life, our jour - ney and our end,
shim - mer - ing stars, im - men - si - ty of space,
as faith - ful stew - ards of the land and air.
to seek with - in each life the spark di - vine;

in - dwell our spir - its through these earth - ly days that
ten - der - est blos - som, maj - es - ty of trees, deep
Through beau - ty's long - ing, mys - ter - y pro - found, show
all of us kin - folk in Thy fam - i - ly, drawn

eve - ry breath may be a hymn of praise.
roll - ing splen - dor of sun - paint - ed seas.
us that all the earth is ho - ly ground.
to each oth - er by our love for Thee.

Patricia V. Long

Mwamba ni Yesu
(The Rock is Jesus)

Original Swahili text: Manaseh G. Mutsoli
English text: J. Nathan Corbitt

MWAMBA
Irregular

from *Four African Hymns*
Copyright © 1994 Choristers Guild
Used by permission.

Traditional Swahili chorus
arr. J. Nathan Corbitt

NOTE: see Psalm 136 for percussion parts

Psalm 136

Original Swahili text: Mwalimu Glen T. Boyd
English text: C. Michael Hawn

KIHAYA
Irregular

Kihaya melody
arr. Mwalimu Glen T. Boyd and J. Nathan Corbitt

8

The redeemed praise

V. Michael McKay

1988

REDEEMED PRAISE
6.7

1. If You had not saved me, I don't know where I would be.
2. Through storm clouds, through dark clouds, the Son will al - ways shine through.
3. I'm grate - ful, so grate - ful; I'm grate - ful, Mas - ter to You.

© 1988 Shaff Music Publishing
Used by permission.

V. Michael McKay

9

Call to worship

Spirit of the living God, discover us today. Come through the tangled path-ways, grown with weed and thicket, that have kept us from you. We cannot reach you; reach to us, that some soul who came here barren of your grace may go out singing, O God, you are my God. **Amen.**

Harry Emerson Fosdick

Harry Emerson Fosdick, "Spirit of the Living God, Discover Us Today," in *Harry Emerson Fosdick: Preacher, Pastor, Prophet* by Robert Moats Miller (New York: Oxford University Press, 1985). Used by permission.

In this place

1992

V. Michael McKay

IN THIS PLACE
Irregular

This is the place; now is the time; we are the peo-

ple Je-sus had in mind. We're gath-ered in this place, at this ap-point-ed time.

We've come to pray; let's get Je - sus on our minds.

V. Michael McKay

11 *We, O God, unite our voices*

Paul Duke and Grady Nutt   1981   HYFRYDOL
87.87 D

1. We, O God, u-nite our voi-ces, raised in thank-ful
2. See-ing then the task be-fore us bind our hearts and
3. Not our choice the wind's di-rec-tion, un-for-seen the

praise to Thee. Thou, un-chan-ging, safe hath brought us
hands as one. May our la-bor be in un-ion.
calm or gale. Thy great o-cean swells be-fore us,

through the ev-er-chan-ging sea. Days of calm and days of
Our re-solve and Thine be one. With one spir-it let us
and our ship seems small and frail. Fierce and gleam-ing is Thy

con-flict, nights of dark-ness prove Thy grace. Hands be-neath us,
la-bor toward the bright ho-ri-zon far. In the midst of
my-st'ry draw-ing us to shores un-known: plunge us on with

Rowland H. Prichard; harm. from *English Hymnal*

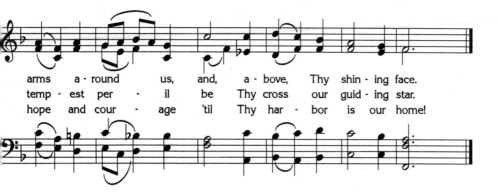

arms	a - round	us,	and,	a - bove,	Thy	shin - ing face.
temp - est	per - il	be	Thy	cross	our	guid - ing star.
hope	and cour - age	'til	Thy	har - bor	is	our home!

Call to worship 12

Leader: Eternal God, high above all,
your children gather in your sanctuary
to worship you.

Men: You fill the heaven and the earth
so that none can hide where you cannot see.

Women: Through all the universe you flow
like living blood through our bodies,
Yet there is one spot where we feel the pulse,
where putting the finger, we know the heart is beating.

Leader: Let your sanctuary be that to us this day.

All: **O God, who fills all things,**
here let us feel the beating of the Eternal Heart. Amen.

Harry Emerson Fosdick

Harry Emerson Fosdick, "Eternal God, High Above All," in *Harry Emerson Fosdick: Preacher, Pastor, Prophet* by Robert Moats Miller
New York: Oxford University Press, 1985). Used by permission.

13 *If it had not been for the Lord*

Margaret P. Douroux   1980   DOUROUX
Irregular

Margaret Pleasant Douroux

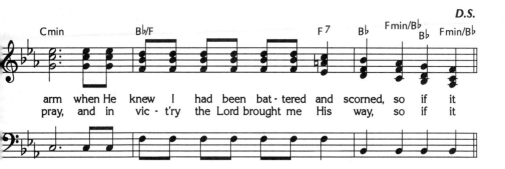

arm when He knew I had been bat - tered and scorned, so if it
pray, and in vic - t'ry the Lord brought me His way, so if it

Prayer of praise 14

Leader: Most High, All Powerful, God of Goodness;
  To you be praise and glory,
    honor and all thankfulness.
  To you alone, Most High, are these things due,
    and no person is worthy to speak of you.
Men: Be praised, O God, for all your creation,
  More especially for our Brother the Sun,
    who brings forth the day and gives light thereby.
  For the Sun is glorious and splendid in its radiance,
    and to you, O God, the Sun bears similitude.
Women: Be praised, O God, for our Sister the Moon,
    and for the Stars in the heavens.
  You have set them bright and sparkling and beautiful.
Men: Be praised, O God, for our brother the Wind,
    for the air and for the clouds,
    for the serene and tempestuous days,
    for through these you sustain all living things.
Women: Be praised, O God, for our Sister the Water,
    for she gives boundless service,
    and is lowly, precious and pure.
Men: Be praised, O God, for our Brother the Fire,
    through whom you give light in the night hours,
    for Fire is beautiful and joyous, vigorous and strong.
Women: Be praised, O God, for our Sister Mother Earth,
    who nourishes us and rules over us,
    and brings forth diverse fruit,
    and bright flowers and herbs.
All: **Be praised and blessed, O God,**
    in endless thanksgiving,
    and served in all humility. Amen.

St. Francis of Assisi
Adapted from the "Canticle of the Sun"

15 Give thanks for music-making art

Brian Wren

1993

ELLACOMBE
CMD

1. Give thanks for mu - sic-mak - ing art, and praise the Spir - it's
2. Through years of train - ing they ac - crue the skills of mind and
3. With mu - sic, mov - ing on through time in se - quen - ces of
4. Then let us reach for ex - cel - lence to sing and sym - pho -
5. God, give us mu - sic to ex - press and right - ly in - ter -

choice of mem - bers called and set a - part with in - stru - ment and
hand, which hours of prac - tice must re - new, en - liv - en, and ex -
sound, we show and tell God's sto - ry - line of how the lost are
nize for God, our ut - most au - di - ence, with joy our high - est
weave our yearn - ing with our thank - ful - ness, and sing what we be -

voice. With work and wis - dom, skills hard - won, life -
pand. With Spir - it - grace they tune our hopes; to
found; the old, un - fold - ing cov - e - nant of
prize. When kind - ly skills our spir - it lifts and
lieve, till glo - rious in the realms of grace, with

Words: Brian Wren
Words © 1993 by Hope Publishing Company, Carol Stream IL 60188.
All Rights Reserved. Used by permission.

Gesangbuch der H.W.K Hofkapelle

giv - ing and life - long, they cel - e - brate what
Christ their hearts be - long; for love of God must
_ jus - tice right - ing wrong, re - sounds through word and
makes the hum - ble strong, give thanks and praise the
new cre - a - tion's throng, our Sav - ior meets us

God has done, and lead the peo - ple's song.
guide the arts that lead the peo - ple's song.
_ sac - ra - ment, and leads the peo - ple's song.
grace - ful gifts that lead the peo - ple's song.
face to face and leads the peo - ple's song.

Collect for worship   16

O God of ancient prophets and holy martyrs, pour out your spirit upon us in this new day, that once again in the hour of our need we may dream dreams and see visions. Drop the plumbline of your justice beside every wall we have built; weigh in the balances of your truth all the accomplishments of our skill and science; test with your consuming fire the permanent worth of our industry and art. If the earth be shaken, and the foundations tremble, grant us courage to look beyond the ruins to that which has not fallen. If judgment falls, and the hollow vanity of much that passed for the substance of life is revealed as nothing, steady us until we lift up our eyes unto you, and know that our hope is in you, both now and forever. In the name of him who was steadfast against death and sin, we pray for our own perseverance in all good works. **Amen.**

Samuel H. Miller

17 O, when shall I see Jesus?

attr. to John Leland early 19th century THE MORNING TRUMPET
13.11.13.11 with refrain

1. O, when shall I see Je - sus and reign with Him a -
2. Gird on the gos - pel ar - mor of faith and hope and
3. Our ears shall hear with glad - ness the host of heav - en

bove, and shall hear the trum - pet sound in that morn - ing, and
love, and you'll hear the trum - pet sound in that morn - ing. And
sing, and shall hear the trum - pet sound in that morn - ing. Our

from the flow - ing foun - tain drink ev - er - last - ing love, and shall
when the com - bat's end - ed He'll car - ry you a - bove, and you'll
tongues shall speak the glo - ries of our im - mor - tal King, and shall

Refrain

hear the trum - pet sound in that morn - ing? O, shout "glo - ry!" I shall
hear the trum - pet sound in that morn - ing.
hear the trum - pet sound in that morn - ing.

Music arr.: Donald P. Hustad
Harmonization © 1990 Hope Publishing Company, Carol Stream, IL 60188.
All Rights Reserved. Used by permission.

The Sacred Harp; arr. Donald P. Hustad

mount a-bove the skies, when I hear the trum-pet sound in that morn - ing.

We love your world, O God 18

Stephen D. Jones   1991

ST. THOMAS
SM

1. We love your world, O God: the birds and mounds of clay, re-
2. We love your world, O God: its cul-tures' vast ar - ray, dis-
3. We love your world, O God: new part - ners ev - ery day, who
4. We love your world, O God: our hab - i - tat each day, our

spect - ing earth, cre - a - ted whole, re - flects your or - dered way.
tinct in lan - guage, race and hope, re - flects your won - drous way.
lis - ten, learn and seek new truth, re - flect your glo - bal way.
hos - pice to the stran - ger here re - flects your host - ing way.

Words © 1991 Stephen D. Jones
Used by permission.

Aaron Williams, *The New Universal Psalmist*

19 Our Father God, who art in heaven

Adoniram Judson   1825   MORNING SONG

CM

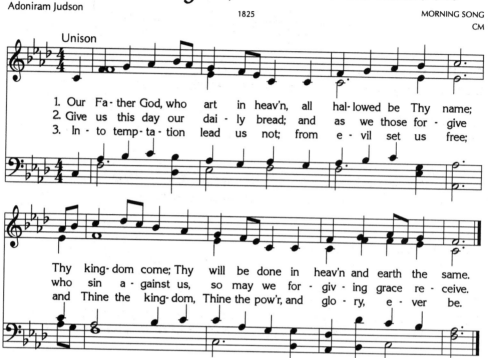

1. Our Fa-ther God, who art in heav'n, all hal-lowed be Thy name;
2. Give us this day our dai-ly bread; and as we those for-give
3. In-to temp-ta-tion lead us not; from e-vil set us free;

Thy king-dom come; Thy will be done in heav'n and earth the same.
who sin a-gainst us, so may we for-giv-ing grace re-ceive.
and Thine the king-dom, Thine the pow'r, and glo-ry, e-ver be.

Traditional American melody, *Kentucky Harmony, Part Second*

20 Collect for worship

Eternal God, when we think of all who counted it not unwise to labor and love beyond all that was asked or expected of them, we grow conscious of the shamefulness of our own meager, careful way of doing good. We are humbled by the memory of men and women whose work made the world in which we live; of those whose tired hands and wearied hearts have carried on in faithfulness; of those handicapped but courageous, desperate but undaunted, mistreated but magnanimous; of all who have cast aside the cautious bookkeeping by which benevolence is scrimped to a profitable venture, and out of their generous faith created wide margins of confidence and freedom for the lives of others. Keep alive in us the faith of those who trusted us and grant us grace to exercise it that it may be the liberation of souls now held in bondage of fear and embarrassment. **Amen.**

Samuel H. Miller

A traditional prayer
in a different voice

Our Father who art in heaven,
Our Creator, you are all around us and within us.

hallowed be thy name.
We praise you with many different names.

Thy kingdom come, thy will be done,
Help us live as we understand we should from knowing you
in harmony and connectedness with each other,

on earth as it is in heaven.
with all creatures of the earth,
and with the earth and the universe itself.

Give us this day our daily bread,
Help us take responsibility when we fail to live harmoniously,
and help us understand and forgive when others let us down.

and forgive us our sins as we forgive those who sin against us.
Help us to use your resources wisely
so that we might be sustained.

And lead us not into temptation,
Let us know you well enough that we are not tempted
to live outside of your love,

but deliver us from evil,
and empower us to work together to overcome evil.

for thine is the kingdom and the power and the glory forever.
We believe that you created the world
and that you will be all around us and within us forever.

Amen.
We are open to you.

Lyn Seils Robertson

22 How can I keep from singing?

(My life flows on)

Anonymous

1869

HOW CAN I KEEP FROM SINGING

87.87 with refrain

1. My life flows on in end-less song, a-bove earth's lam-en-ta-tion. I
2. Through all the tu-mult and the strife, I hear that mu-sic ring-ing. It
3. What though my joys and com-forts die? The Lord my Sav-ior liv-eth. What
4. The peace of Christ makes fresh my heart, a foun-tain ev-er spring-ing! All

hear the real, though far-off hymn that hails a new cre-a-tion.
finds an ech-o in my soul. How can I keep from sing-ing?
though the dark-ness gath-er 'round? Songs in the night He giv-eth.
things are mine since I am His! How can I keep from sing-ing?

Refrain

No storm can shake my in-most calm while to that Rock I'm cling-ing. Since

love is Lord of heav'n and earth, how can I keep from sing-ing?

Robert Lowry, *Bright Jewels for the Sunday School,* 1869

O God, in restless living

Harry Emerson Fosdick   1931   RUTHERFORD
76.76.76.75

1. O God, in rest-less liv-ing we lose our spir-its peace. Calm our un-wise con-fu-sion, bid Thou our clam-or cease. Let anx-ious hearts grow qui-et, like pools at eve-ning still, till Thy re-flect-ed heav-ens all our spir-its fill.

2. Teach us, be-yond our striv-ing, the rich re-wards of rest. Who does not live se-rene-ly is nev-er deep-ly bless'd. O tran-quil, ra-diant sun-light, bring Thou our lives to flow'r, less wea-ried with our ef-fort, more a-ware of pow'r.

3. Re-cep-tive make our spir-its, our need is to be still. As dawn fades flick-'ring can-dle, so dim our anx-ious will. Re-veal Thy ra-diance through us, Thine am-ple strength re-lease. Not ours, but Thine the tri-umph in the pow'r of peace.

4. We grow not wise by strug-gling, we gain but things by strain. We cease to wa-ter gar-dens, when comes Thy plen-teous rain. O, beau-ti-fy our spir-its in rest-ful-ness from strife, en-rich our souls in se-cret with a-bun-dant life.

Edward F. Rimbault

24 When sorrow floods the troubled heart

Rebecca Turner Lawson and Paul Duke 1989 KINGSFOLD
CMD

1. When sor-row floods the trou-bled heart and clouds the mind with
2. The voice is stilled, no words ex-press the pain that lin-gers
3. The sting of death can-not for-bid the child of God to

fears, af-flic-tion pres-ses from the soul the bit-ter flow of
on; our prayer be-comes a si-lent sigh; all mor-tal speech is
sing. The scars we bear may long re-main, but res-ur-rec-tion

tears. God's weep-ing chil-dren raise the prayer: "Al-migh-ty God, how
gone. Then Ho-ly Spir-it groans in us with in-ter-ces-sion
brings the heal-ing of the bro-ken heart, the right-ing of the

long till tears shall cease and si-lence break and grief be turned to song?"
strong; when tears have ceased and si-lence breaks the Spir-it stirs a song.
wrong. Our tears shall cease, our si-lence break in Christ, the liv-ing Song.

arr. Ralph Vaughan Williams

Only You, O Lord

Andreas Sudarsono
translation and arrangement: William N. McElrath   1977

HANYA PADAMU, TUHAN
4.6.9 D with refrain

1. When storm winds blow and clouds made dark my day, I run to
   surge and sweep a - cross my way, I lean for
2. Be- cause of You, O Lord, my soul is bright: Your glo - ry
   me, O Lord, in dark - est night, when sor - row

You for shel - ter, O Lord; when storm waves
strength up - on You, O Lord.
shines on each step I take; You com - fort
makes my sad heart to break.

Refrain

On - ly You, O Lord my God! I hang my hopes, my hopes on You. Yes, on-ly

You, O Lord my God! I yield my life, my life to You.

Andreas Sudarsono

26 *In these dark uncertain moments*

João Fernandes da Silva Neto
English translation: Joan R. Sutton

1987/1994

ECOLOGIA
87.87 D

1. In these dark, un-cer-tain mo-ments of con-fu-sion, doubt and fear, when de-struc-tion, wars and fam-ine threat-en all that we hold dear, hear our prayer, O God, our Fa-ther, show your mer-cy from a-bove; give us homes firm-ly con-struc-ted on your strong and per-fect love.

2. In these days so full of e-vil, dis-re-spect, dis-trust and greed, we for-get to look a-round us, to reach out to those in need. Hear our prayer, dear Lord in Hea-ven, help us show our love for you; give us homes full of com-pas-sion, that are faith-ful, kind and true.

3. In your name we trust, Lord Je-sus, in your wis-dom, in your might; make our homes a sweet com-mu-nion full of peace, good-will, and light. Hear our prayer, O Lord, and give us your for-give-ness and your grace. Help our fa-thers, mo-thers, child-ren to re-flect your lov-ing face.

João Fernandes da Silva Neto

A litany:
O God of all the children

O God of the children of Somalia, Sarajevo,
   South Africa and South Carolina,
  of Albania, Alabama, Bosnia and Boston,
  of Cracow and Cairo, Chicago and Croatia,
Help us to love and respect and protect them all.

O God of black and brown and white and Albino Children
   and those all mixed together,
  of children who are rich and poor and in between,
  of children who speak English and Russian and Hmong
   and languages our ears cannot discern,
Help us to love and respect and protect them all.

O God of the child prodigy and child prostitute,
  of the child of rapture and the child of rape,
  of run or thrown away children who struggle every day
   without parent or place or friend or future,
Help us to love and respect and protect them all.

O God of children who can walk and talk
  and hear and see
  and sing and dance
  and jump and play
  and of children who wish they could but can't,
  of children who are loved and unloved, wanted and unwanted,
Help us to love and respect and protect them all.

O God of beggar, beaten, abused, neglected, AIDS,
   drug and hunger-ravaged children,
  of children who are emotionally fragile,
  of children who rebel and ridicule, torment and taunt,
Help us to love and respect and protect them all.

O God of children of destiny and of despair,
  of war and of peace,
  of disfigured, diseased and dying children,
  of children without hope
  and of children with hope to spare and share,
Help us to love and respect and protect them all.

Marian Wright Edelman

Give me a clean heart

Margaret J. Douroux

1970

CLEAN HEART
Irregular

Give me a clean heart so I may

serve Thee. Lord fix my heart so that I may be

Margaret J. Douroux

29 The Lord is my shepherd

Lucie E. Campbell

1919

CAMPBELL
Irregular

1. The Lord is my Shep-herd, I shall not want; by still wa-ters He lead-eth His sheep; tho' the en-e-my gath-er and foes may op-press, Je-sus watch-es while His lit-tle ones sleep.

2. He mak-eth me to lie down in pas-tures green, my cup with His bless-ings o-ver-flows; He a-noint-eth my head with oil from a-bove, for my Mas-ter has boun-ti-ful stores.

3. He pre-par-eth a ta-ble in the midst of my foes, but His good-ness and mer-cy are there; at the end of death's val-ley, in the house of the Lord, there for-ev-er His good-ness we'll share.

Refrain

We will

Christian F. Witt; adapted by Henry Gauntlett

walk thro' the val-ley, we will walk in peace; we will walk thro' the

val-ley with Je-sus a-lone; on His rod and His staff thro' the

val-ley of death, we will walk thro' the val-ley in peace.

Psalm 51

Paraphrased by Darrell Adams

1977/1994

PSALM 51
Irregular

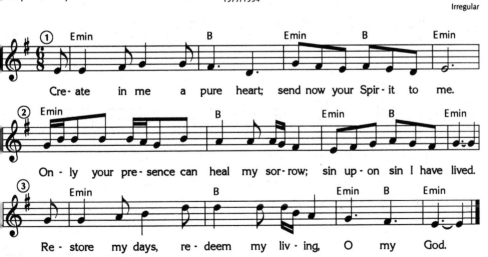

Cre-ate in me a pure heart; send now your Spir-it to me.

On-ly your pre-sence can heal my sor-row; sin up-on sin I have lived.

Re-store my days, re-deem my liv-ing, O my God.

Darrell Adams

may be sung as a canon

31

Congregational prayer
of confession

O God of mystery and love,
>   whose grace is so abundantly bestowed on us,
>   thank you for Jesus Christ who unites all people and all things.
We confess as individuals, and as a congregation,
>   that we are often engaged in actions that separate.

We confess, O God, that we are often uncomfortable
>   **with the thought of being united with some people.**
We do not want to walk among the poor and the homeless.
We are reluctant to care, to tend those
>   **whose diseases might affect us.**
We often insulate ourselves from people
>   **who remind us of our own mortality**
>   **and the transience of the life we know.**
Our fear prevents us from making our world
>   **more like your kingdom.**
Our fear prevents us from opening our hearts and our souls
>   **so that your kingdom might form within each of us.**
Forgive us.
Help us to make room in our hearts
>   **that you may form your image within us,**
>   **and that our every impulse and action might lead**
>   **to the coming of your kingdom in this world. Amen.**

Kathy Manis Findley

Prayer against war

O Lord, since first the blood of Abel cried to you
    from the ground that drank it,
    your earth has been defiled with the blood
    shed by his brother's hand,
    and the centuries sob with the ceaseless horror of war.
Ever the pride of kings and the covetousness of the strong
    have driven peaceful nations to slaughter.
Ever the songs of the past and the pomp of armies
    have been used to inflame the passions of the people.
Our spirit cries out to you in revolt against it, and we know
    that our righteous anger is answered by your holy wrath.
Break the spell of the enchantments that make the nations drunk
    with the lust of battle and draw them on as willing tools of death.
Grant us a quiet and steadfast mind
    when our own nation clamors for vengeance or aggression.
Strengthen our sense of justice and our regard for the equal worth
    of other peoples and races.
Grant to the rulers of nations faith
    in the possibility of peace through justice,
    and grant to the common people a new and stern
    enthusiasm for the cause of peace.
Teach our age nobler methods of matching our strength
    and more effective ways of giving our life for the flag.
O God of all nations, draw all your great family together with an
    increasing sense of our common blood and destiny,
    that peace may come on earth at last,
    and your sun may shed its light rejoicing
    on a holy communion of people. Amen.

Walter Rauschenbusch

Adapted from *Prayers of the Social Awakening* by Walter Rauschenbusch (New York: The Pilgrim Press, 1910).

Christ, our liberty

Peggy Haymes

1993

NETTLETON
87.87D

1. Once a peo-ple came to-geth-er bound by faith and vi-sion
2. Hav-ing suff-ered per-se-cu-tion, they now fought for free-dom's
3. From our sin our Lord has freed us; in our dark-ness light has
4. In our free-dom God com-mands us that we share God's gift of

new; with the won - der of the gos - pel came God's
cause, that our faith be free - ly cho - sen not de -
shined. In our pain our Lord brings heal - ing words of
grace; for the sake of God's cre - a - tion, we seek

gift of free-dom true. Freed to fol - low Christ in
fined by hu-man laws. We their child - ren are en -
hope for hu-man-kind. Still so ma - ny live in
vi - sion for this day. Like our fa - thers and our

ser - vice, freed to wor - ship and to seek; con-science
trust - ed with the dream they dared to dream; each one
sha - dows, hun - ger, hate, grief and des - pair. Some for -
mo - thers, may we al - ways faith-ful be; in our

Wyeth's *Repository of Sacred Music, Part Second*, 1813

guid - ed by God's spir - it, God their sole au - thor - i - ty.
free to seek God's lead - ing, in our Lord our un - i - ty.
got - ten, some un - no - ticed, some un - touched by hands of care.
dy - ing find our li - ving, bound to Christ, our Li - ber - ty.

Litany for religious liberty 34

Baptists have never been party to oppression of conscience.

**Our contention is not for more toleration,
but for absolute liberty.**

There is a wide difference between toleration and liberty.

Toleration implies that someone falsely claims the right to tolerate.

Toleration is a concession, while liberty is a right.

**Toleration is a matter of expediency,
while liberty is a matter of principle.**

Toleration is a gift from people,
while liberty is a gift from God.

**It is the consistent and insistent contention of our Baptist people,
always and everywhere,
that religion must be forever voluntary and uncoerced.**

And that it is not the prerogative of any power,
whether civil or ecclesiastical,
to compel anyone to conform to any religious creed of worship.

God wants free worshipers and no other kind.

George W. Truett

Adapted from "Baptists and Religious Liberty" by George W. Truett. Delivered on the steps of the United States Capitol building, May 16, 1920.

35 O Lord, who gave us freedom's theme

William R. Hornbuckle

1986/1993

FOREST GREEN
CMD

1. O Lord, who gave us free-dom's theme and said that truth would be the
2. In cre - a - tiv - i - ty, O Lord, you made us with true worth; your
3. Where no - ble ends make just the means to which the crowd as - pires, give
4. When sa - cred theme and pa - triot scheme are blurred and merged to one, give
5. Should ap - a - thy and com-fort lull our con - science in - to rest; re-

means by which we would in - deed know full - est lib - er - ty; keep
crowned cre - a - tion, giv - en thus do - min - ion of the Earth. You
us the will our for-bears had to bright - en free-dom's fires; to
us the clear - er vi - sion still to say, "Thy will be done." The
new in us the cen - tral truths of faith's au - then - tic test: a

press - ing us to search for truth with heal - thy pi - e - ty. May
gave us life, and grant - ed us the el - e - ment of choice; to
cau - tion those who in your name stamp out di - ver - si - ty; to
land to which we give our oath can nev - er tru - ly be a
jus - tice done, a mer - cy loved, a ser - vant's san - dals shod; true

we not rest un - til we've shared the fruits of be - ing free.
you we turn for free-dom's sake, to you we lift our voice.
set at lib - er - ty the mind where think - ing is - n't free.
sub - sti - tute for free-dom's goal: "All na - tions un - der Thee."
sub - jects then, we will sal - ute the king - dom of our God.

English melody arr. Ralph Vaughan Williams

Litany in celebration of religious liberty

Leader I: Magistrates are not by virtue of their office to meddle with religion or matters of conscience, to force or compel people to this or that form of religion. (John Smyth, 1612)

People: **We rejoice in our freedom**
and accept the charge to live faithfully within it.

Leader II: No king nor bishop can or is able to command faith. That is the gift of God. To constrain princes and peoples to receive the one true religion of the gospel is wholly against the mind and merciful law of Christ. (Leonard Busher, 1614)

People: **We rejoice in our freedom**
and accept the charge to live faithfully within it.

Leader I: Every person ought to be left free with respect to matters of religion. The Holy Author of our religion needs no compulsive measures for the promotion of God's cause.
(General Committee of Baptists in Virginia, 1785)

People: **We rejoice in our freedom**
and accept the charge to live faithfully within it.

Leader II: Everyone must give a personal account to God, and therefore all people ought to be at liberty to serve God in a way that each can best reconcile to [their] own conscience.
(John Leland, 1791)

People: **We rejoice in our freedom**
and accept the charge to live faithfully within it.

Leader I: Religion must be forever voluntary and uncoerced. It is not the prerogative of any power to compel people to conform to any religious creed or form of worship, or to worship, or to pay taxes for the support of a creed they do not believe. God wants free worshipers and no other kind. (George W. Truett, 1920)

People: **We rejoice in our freedom**
and accept the charge to live faithfully within it.

Leader II: Baptists believe in free churches within a free state. We believe religious liberty to be an inalienable human right and indispensable to human welfare. Profoundly convinced that any deprivation of this right is a wrong to be challenged, we condemn every form of compulsion or restraint in religion.
(The American Baptist Bill of Rights, 1939)

People: **We rejoice in our freedom**
and accept the charge to live faithfully within it.

Compiled by Reid Trulson

37 *Evergreen and ever-fragrant*

Philip M. Young   1992   STUTTGART
87.87

1. Ev-er-green and ev-er-fra-grant sym-bol of e-ter-ni-ty,
2. Light of lights to all de-scend-ing, white of per-fect pur-i-ty,
3. Star and creche and her-ald an-gel tell of love and mys-ter-y,
4. Cross of sac-ri-fice and suff-'ring, crown of life and vic-to-ry,

tell-ing of the Christ with-in us, stands the won-drous Chris-mon tree.
gold of maj-es-ty and glo-ry crown the ra-diant Chris-mon tree.
cel-e-brate the Christ a-mong us, wel-comed by the Chris-mon tree.
Je-sus Christ our Lord re-veal-ing: hon-ored through the Chris-mon tree.

Christian F. Witt; adapted by Henry Gauntlett

38 *In ancient times the people yearned*

Milburn Price   1989   ST. ANNE
CM

1. In an-cient times the peo-ple yearned, in dark-ness as the
2. You came, O Christ, to preach good news to those in mis-er-
3. When your re-demp-tive work was done ac-cord-ing to God's
4. We wait, O Lord, for your re-turn! From now un-til that

night, to see ful-filled the pro-phe-cy, the com-ing of the light.
y, to of-fer hope to those who mourn, to set the cap-tives free.
plan, at your a-scent a pro-mise came, that you would come a-gain.
day may we have faith to live in hope and fol-low in your way.

attr. to William Croft

The peaceable kingdom

What is peace?

Peace is a condition which delivers
both oppressor and oppressed,
both hunter and hunted,
both victor and victim
from the terrors of violent death
and frees them to enter the kingdom
of a common life.

"The wolf shall lie down with the lamb,
and the leopard shall lie down with the kid,
and the calf and the lion and the fatling together." (Isaiah 11:6)

Is it practical nonsense to think about and pray for a day when
we shall stop killing each other and one another's children,
and begin caring for each other?

Is it pure visionary fuzzy-headedness to believe in God
and that God will never accept an arrangement
in which some are exploiters and oppressors
while others are exploited and oppressed?

Is it possible in the face of global nuclear catastrophe
to cling to Isaiah's vision of "the Peaceable Kingdom"?

We must cherish it or become hopeless.

If God is God, someday Isaiah's vision,
shared by all God-loving persons on earth,
must come to pass.

The vision declares, "They shall not hurt or destroy
in all my holy mountain." (Isaiah 11:9)

The hurting and destroying must stop.
Lord God, hasten that day's coming
and make us instruments of Your peace.

L.D. Johnson

L.D. Johnson, "What is Peace? (The Peaceable Kingdom)," adapted from *Images of Eternity* (Nashville: Broadman Press, 1984), pp. 60-61.
Used by permission.

40 The Lord has made me with dignity

Jack Bruce 1990

DIGNITY
Irregular

1. The Lord has made me with dig-ni-ty, gave me worth and in-teg-ri-ty. I am cre-a-ted free and e-qual, made to be like God. For I am made in the im-age of God, and I am beau-ti-ful in this Light! For I am made in the I am beau-ti-ful in this Light!

2. The Lord has made you with dig-ni-ty, gave you worth and in-teg-ri-ty. You are cre-a-ted free and e-qual, made to be like God. For you are made in the im-age of God, and you are beau-ti-ful in this Light! For you are made in the You are beau-ti-ful in this Light!

For I am made, For I am I am made in the im-age of God. made in this Light! For I am made, I am made in the

For you are made, for you are You are made in the im-age of God. made in this Light! For you are made, You are made in the

Jack Bruce; arr. C. Michael Hawn

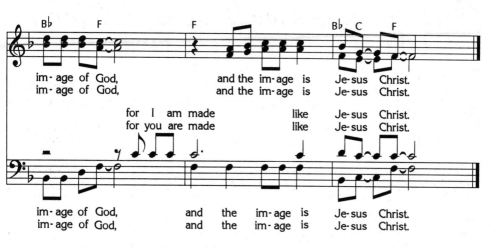

im-age of God, and the im-age is Je-sus Christ.
im-age of God, and the im-age is Je-sus Christ.

for I am made like Je-sus Christ.
for you are made like Je-sus Christ.

im-age of God, and the im-age is Je-sus Christ.
im-age of God, and the im-age is Je-sus Christ.

Stanza 3: substitute "us" for "me" and "we" for "I"
Stanza 4: substitute "them" for "me" and "they" for "I"

Liberty, that sweet word sounding [41]

Frances S. Dean

1986

STUTTGART
87.87

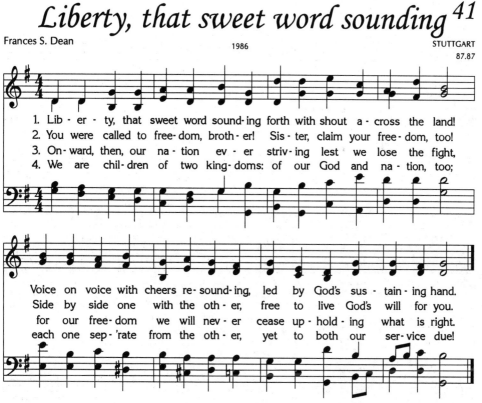

1. Lib - er - ty, that sweet word sound-ing forth with shout a - cross the land!
2. You were called to free-dom, broth-er! Sis - ter, claim your free - dom, too!
3. On-ward, then, our na - tion ev - er striv-ing lest we lose the fight,
4. We are chil-dren of two king-doms: of our God and na - tion, too;

Voice on voice with cheers re-sound-ing, led by God's sus - tain - ing hand.
Side by side one with the oth - er, free to live God's will for you.
for our free-dom we will nev - er cease up - hold - ing what is right.
each one sep - 'rate from the oth - er, yet to both our ser - vice due!

Christian F. Witt; adapted by Henry Gauntlett

Eternal God
whose searching eye doth scan

Edwin McNeill Poteat   c. 1948   OIKOUMENIKOS
10.10.10.10

1. E - ter - nal God whose search - ing eye doth scan
2. Help us to see the king - dom of Thy Son
3. Bright - en the light that shines up - on our day,
4. Strike from our souls the fet - ters of our fears;

a - ges and climes no lim - its can con - fine;
wid - er than na - tion, deep - er still than race;
gird with Thy love the weak - ness of our creeds;
lev - el the bar - riers of the nar - row mind,

broad - en thy vis - tas in our eyes to - day
chast - en our joy in mea - ger vic - t'ries won;
teach us to trust our fel - lows in the way;
ad - vance Thy church through - out the com - ing years

till we shall share the vi - sion that is thine.
'stab - lish our go - ings in a broad - er place.
give us the faith that con - quers and con - cedes.
wide as the world and broad as hu - man - kind.

Words and Music by Edward McNeill Poteat   Edwin McNeill Poteat

Alternate Tune: MORECAMBE

Proclamation of good news 43
for women

On March 23-27, 1992, women from twenty countries (including Sri Lanka, Korea, India, El Salvador, and Nigeria) met in Swanwick, Derbyshire, England, to address the needs of women around the world. The following Proclamation, reprinted with permission, is the outgrowth of the first Women's Global Consultation on Evangelism sponsored by the Women's Department of the Baptist World Alliance:

The Gospel of Jesus Christ is good news to all the women of the world.
To those who are weighed down with guilt, it is forgiveness.
To those who sin, it is redemption and renewal.
To those who are oppressed, it is freedom.
To those who live with fear, it is peace.
To those who are despised and rejected, it is kinship with the God
who endured the shame of the Cross.
To those who are bound by culture and tradition,
it is emancipation by One who treated women as equals.
To those who cannot trust, it is dependence upon One
who has proven Himself trustworthy.
To those who are lonely, it is friendship with the Best Friend
women ever had.
To those who are devalued,
it is a new identity as joint-heirs of the grace of God.

Women:
As women who follow the Lord Jesus Christ,
we are compelled by His love, commanded by His Word,
and gifted by His Spirit to share this Gospel
with those who have not seen or heard
the salvation of our God.
Therefore, we will radiate His light into the dark corners
of women's experience;
We will bear His life to those who are dying;
We will share our bread with those who are hungry;
We will declare His promise of resurrection
to those who are powerless;
We will bring affirmation to those
who do not know they are made in the image of God.

All:
We will see with the eyes of Jesus, weep with His tears,
hear with His ears, speak with His words,
touch with His hands, embrace with His arms,
and feel with His heart until that great day comes
when every woman, man, and child
will know the glorious grace and goodness of our God.

44 *We stand united in the truth*

Philip M. Young   1986   ELLACOMBE
CMD

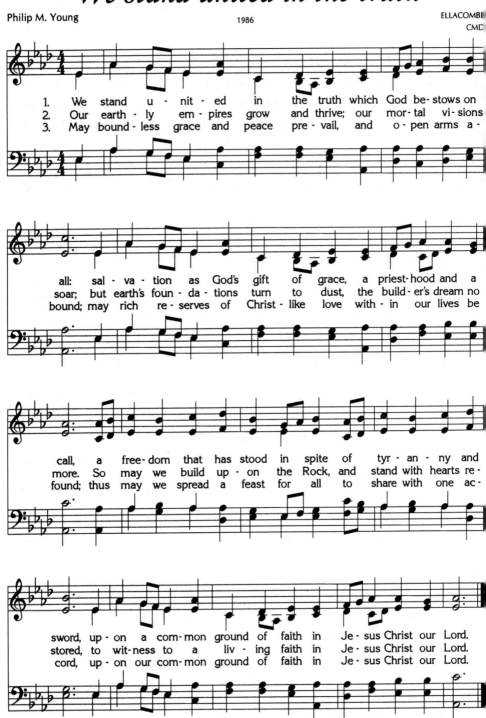

1. We stand u-nit-ed in the truth which God be-stows on all: sal-va-tion as God's gift of grace, a priest-hood and a call, a free-dom that has stood in spite of tyr-an-ny and sword, up-on a com-mon ground of faith in Je-sus Christ our Lord.

2. Our earth-ly em-pires grow and thrive; our mor-tal vi-sions soar; but earth's foun-da-tions turn to dust, the build-er's dream no more. So may we build up-on the Rock, and stand with hearts re-stored, to wit-ness to a liv-ing faith in Je-sus Christ our Lord.

3. May bound-less grace and peace pre-vail, and o-pen arms a-bound; may rich re-serves of Christ-like love with-in our lives be found; thus may we spread a feast for all to share with one ac-cord, up-on our com-mon ground of faith in Je-sus Christ our Lord.

Gesangbuch der H.W.K Hofkapelle

Jacob wrestling

Thomas A. Jackson

1991

HOLY MANNA
87.87 D

1. Ja - cob wrest - ling with a stran - ger in the dark - ness of the night,
2. We like Ja - cob, too, must strug - gle, grap - ple with our doubts and fears,
3. In the dark - ness we see sha - dows, hear strange voi - ces, feel deep pain,

yield - ing not with - out a bless - ing, grap-pling till the dawn of light.
bit - ter though may be the bat - tle, marked by ag - o - ny and tears.
pray for light to see more clear - ly, fear - ing that we strive in vain.

Though the strug-gle left him wound - ed, Ja - cob knew he had found grace;
Yet that strug-gle can yield bless - ing, doubts de - stroy and fears e - rase,
Yet if we by faith still wres - tle, so our dark - ness will be past;

limp - ing now but healed in spir - it, he had seen God face to face.
though we bear the scars of suff - 'ring bet - ter shall we know God's grace.
in the light that then a - waits us, we will see God's face at last!

Columbian Harmony; attr. to William Moore, compiler

Ordained of God

Edward A. McDowell, Jr.
stanza 4: Randall Lolley and Robert Mullinax

1954/1987

GERMANY
LM

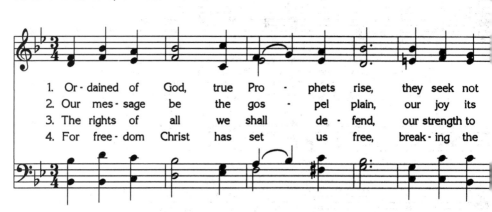

1. Or - dained of God, true Pro - phets rise, they seek not
2. Our mes - sage be the gos - pel plain, our joy its
3. The rights of all we shall de - fend, our strength to
4. For free - dom Christ has set us free, break - ing the

gain nor earth - ly prize, they heed the chal - lenge
pow'r o'er sin's dark stain; born from a - bove the
jus - tice ev - er lend, the sins of greed of
chains of cap - tiv - i - ty. Bound but to God we

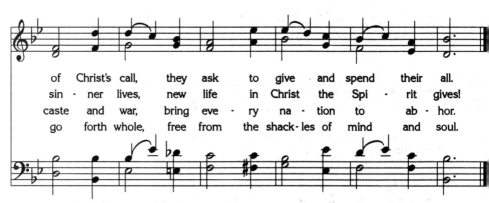

of Christ's call, they ask to give and spend their all.
sin - ner lives, new life in Christ the Spi - rit gives!
caste and war, bring eve - ry na - tion to ab - hor.
go forth whole, free from the shack - les of mind and soul.

Stanzas 1-3 Edward A. McDowell, Jr.
Stanza 4 © 1987 Randall Lolley and Robert Mullinax
Used by permission.

William Gardiner's *Sacred Melodies*

Arise! Servants of Christ, arise!

47

Harold E. Pinkston, Sr.

1986

PROGRESSIVE BAPTIST CHORAL
SMD

1. Ser-vants of Christ a-rise and put your cour-age on. Join
2. *Pro-gress* can sure-ly come through Je-sus' pow'r and love. Stand
3. Hun-ger and greed will cease; the rac-ist pow'r will fade. Pride,
4. *Pro-gress* through *Peace* and love will con-quer death and sin. We

in the cause in sweet ac-cord to end the night of wrong. Strong
fast in *Ser-vice* for the right with strength and grace from God. When
pov-er-ty, and na-ked-ness, when sin has seen its day. God's
yield our souls to Christ, our Lord, who makes us one in Him. His

in the Lord of hope and in His sav-ing power, join
all vic-t'ries are won and eve-ry con-flict passed, the
cause will not be lost; His Spir-it bids us "Come"; then
grace, His Peace, His love be ours for-ev-er-more. To

in the *Fel-low-ship* of Christ, who calls you in this hour.
Peace through Je-sus Christ a-lone will be the world's at last.
Je-sus will de-scend from heav'n and take His ser-vants home.
God all-wise be glo-ry now, through Je-sus Christ, our Lord.

Jean Michael Sebring
and Harold E. Pinkston, Sr.

Alternate Tune: DIADEMATA

48 We now disclaim the power of death

Anna York

1992

EIN' FESTE BURG
87.87.66.667

1. We now dis-claim the power of death that holds our cit-ies
2. Be-hold, O Lord, our cit-ies' plight, the wea-pons, gangs, and
3. We've paid the price in blood and fire for years of a-pa-
4. O God, new vi-sion now im-part to meet the chal-lenge

locked in strife; and we pro-claim the sav-ing name of
sense-less crime; our hun-ger, pov-er-ty, des-pair, our
thy and pride; the bro-ken lives be-fore our eyes de-
of this hour; in-fuse your wis-dom in our plans for

Him who holds the power of life. It's Je-sus Christ, our
chil-dren mur-dered in their prime. Our fear and hate have
mand the truth we've long de-nied: be-neath our va-ried
strug-gling souls to be em-pow-ered. Lord, cleanse our hearts and

Lord, whose migh-ty sav-ing Word re-
wrought in-jus-tice, greed and fraud; hope
skin we all are hu-man kin; one
minds of shame-ful, ra-cial pride; break

Words © 1992 Anna York
Used by permission.

Martin Luther

bukes	the	Strong	Man's	claim	and	breaks	the	cap -	tive's
dims	and	dis -	ap -	pears;	de -	feat	dries	help -	less
blood,	one	breath	we	share;	life's	bur -	dens	we	all
down	the	walls	of	fear,	make	words	and	ac -	tions

chain;	the	poor	and	weak	He	res -	cues.
tears;	Lord,	come	to	save	our	cit -	ies.
bear;	by	one	God	we're	cre - a -	ted.
clear;	cause	us	to	love	each	oth -	er.

The open Bible 49

The open Bible on the pulpit is a testimony to our belief in the presence of God through the proclaimed word and our commitment to the "soul liberty" of the individual conscience. These twin commitments constitute a rich heritage, a present enjoyment, and a treasured legacy for succeeding generations.

From the Sunday bulletin of the First Baptist Church, Providence, Rhode Island, the oldest Baptist congregation in America, founded by Roger Williams in 1638.

50 *Deep in the shadows of the past*

Brian Wren

1973/1993

KINGSFOLD
CMD

1. Deep in the shad-ows of the past, far out from set-tled lands, some no-mads tra-veled with their God a-cross the de-sert sands. The dawn-ing hope of hu-man-kind by them was sensed and shown; a pro-mise call-ing them a-head, a fu-ture yet un-known.

2. While o-thers bowed to change-less gods they met a mys-ter-y, in-vis-i-ble, with-out a name: "I AM WHAT I WILL BE"; and by their tents, a-round their fires, in stor-y, song and law, they praised, re-mem-bered, hand-ed on, a past that pro-mised more.

3. From Ex-o-dus to Pent-e-cost the pro-mise changed and grew, while some, re-mem-ber-ing the past, re-cord-ed what they knew, or with their let-ters and la-ments their pro-phe-cy and praise re-cov-ered, kin-dled and ex-pressed new hope for chang-ing days.

4. For all the writ-ings that sur-vived, for lead-ers, long a-go, who sift-ed, cop-ied and pre-served the Bi-ble that we know, give thanks, and find its sto-ry yet our pro-mise, strength and call, the mo-del of em-er-ging faith, a-live with hope for all.

O God of mercies

Anne Steele

1760

GRÄFENBERG
CM

1. O God of mer - cies, in Thy word
2. Here may the blind and hun - gry come,
3. Here springs of con - so - la - tion rise
4. Here the Re - deem - er's wel - come voice
5. O may these heav'n - ly pa - ges be
6. Di - vine in - struc - tor, gra - cious Lord,

what end - less glo - ry shines! For ev - er be Thy
and light and food re - ceive; here shall the low - liest
to cheer the faint - ing mind; and thir - sty souls re -
spreads hea - v'nly peace a - round; and life and ev - er -
my ev - er - dear de - light; and still new beau - ties
O be for - ev - er near; teach me to love Your

name a - dored for these ce - les - tial lines.
guest have room, and taste and see and live.
ceive sup - plies, and sweet re - fresh - ment find.
last - ing joys at - tend the bliss - ful sound.
may I see, and still in - creas - ing light.
sac - red Word, and view my Sav - ior there.

Johann Crüger

52

Ye people of the north

Anne Skinner

1967

YE PEOPLE
66.86

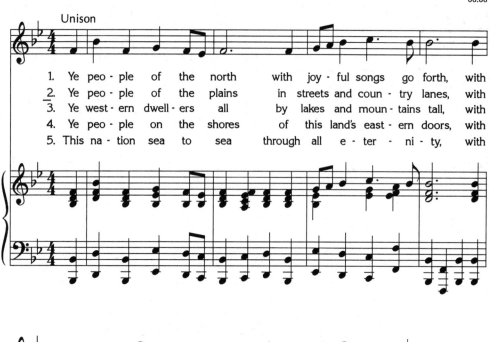

Unison

1. Ye peo-ple of the north with joy-ful songs go forth, with
2. Ye peo-ple of the plains in streets and coun-try lanes, with
3. Ye west-ern dwell-ers all by lakes and moun-tains tall, with
4. Ye peo-ple on the shores of this land's east-ern doors, with
5. This na-tion sea to sea through all e-ter-ni-ty, with

heart and voice sing out! Re-joice! Pro-claim your Mak-er's worth.
heart and voice sing out! Re-joice! De-clare your Sav-ior reigns.
heart and voice sing out! Re-joice! Make known the Mas-ter's call.
heart and voice sing out! Re-joice! God's Word our faith re-stores.
heart and voice sing out! Re-joice! Christ's love brings li-ber-ty.

Jack Hodd

Together now the bread we break 53

G. Temp Sparkman
1983/1994
ST. ANNE
CM

1. To - ge - ther now the bread we break de - void of pride or boast. To -
2. The bread and cup be - long to Him who first the ta - ble spread. And
3. To - geth - er now we keep the feast, the wor - thy Lamb, to praise. This
4. Earth's stran - gers still Em - ma - us seek; the feast was meant for them. Go

ge - ther now the cup we lift of Christ, the gra - cious host.
as Em - ma - us' stran - gers see in Him, the Liv - ing Bread.
gift of mer - cy now we take; thanks - giv - ings joy - ful raise.
share the bread, ex - tend the cup. The Christ still comes who came.

attr. to William Croft; harm. by W.H. Monk

As he gathered at his table 54

Paul A. Richardson
1986
STUART
87.87

1. As He gath - ered at His ta - ble those who longed to know the way,
2. As He took the towel and ba - sin, not as mas - ter, but as friend,
3. As He blessed the bread and broke it, hu - man need to sat - is - fy,
4. As He took the cup and shared it, tell - ing of the Fa - ther's care,
5. As they sang a hymn to - geth - er, prais - ing Is - rael's sav - ing King,
6. As He went in - to the gar - den pray - ing, "Fa - ther, use Your Son,"
7. Though this feast be one of sym - bols, what we cel - e - brate is real;

Christ pro - claimed a ho - ly mys - tery; still His words call us to - day.
Christ por - trayed the way of ser - vice; still in serv - ing we must bend.
Christ made e - ven trai - tors wel - come; still we ques - tion, "Is it I?"
Christ poured out him - self in prom - ise; still that cov - 'nant we must share.
hearts and voic - es made one mu - sic; still de - liv - 'ring love we sing.
Christ a - lone could know its mean - ing; still we pray, "God's will be done."
still Christ wel - comes to his ta - ble; still Christ serves us at His meal.

Paul A. Richardson

Alternate tune: RATHBURN

55 *From every race, from every clime*

Thomas B. McDormand

ST. PETER
CM

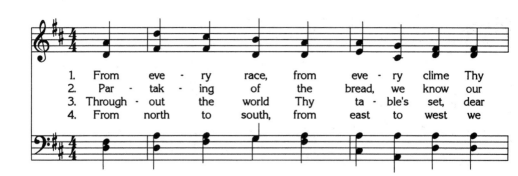

1. From eve - ry race, from eve - ry clime Thy
2. Par - tak - ing of the bread, we know our
3. Through - out the world Thy ta - ble's set, dear
4. From north to south, from east to west we

peo - ple gath - ered 'round the em - blems of Thy
strength from Thee de - rives, and as we take the
Lord, our Sav - ior, guide, in hope we know that
ga - ther to re - call in rev - erent mem - o -

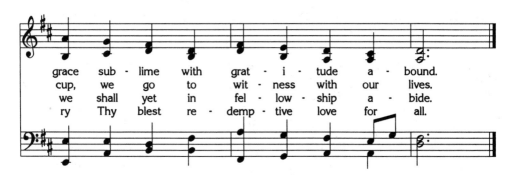

grace sub - lime with grat - i - tude a - bound.
cup, we go to wit - ness with our lives.
we shall yet in fel - low - ship a - bide.
ry Thy blest re - demp - tive love for all.

Alexander R. Reinagle

In water we grow

1989

Brian Wren

LAUDATE DOMINUM
55.55.65.65

1. In wa-ter we grow, se-cure in the womb, and speech-less-ly know love's safe-ty and room. Bap-tiz-ing and bless-ing we pub-lish for good the free-ing, ca-ress-ing safe-keep-ing of God.

2. In wa-ter we wash: the dirt of each day, its trou-ble and rush are car-ried a-way. In Christ re-cre-a-ted by love's cleans-ing art, self-will and self-ha-tred dis-solve and de-part.

3. In wa-ter we dive, and can-not draw breath, then sur-face a-live, re-bound-ing from death. Our old self goes un-der, in Christ dead and drowned. We rise, washed in won-der, by love clad and crowned.

4. In wa-ter we dwell, for by its deep flow through blood-stream and cell, we live, think, and grow. Praise God, love out-flow-ing, whose well of new birth bap-tiz-es our know-ing, and wa-ters the earth.

C. Hubert Parry

Alternate tune: HANOVER

57

Take me to the water

African-American Spiritual with
stanzas 1-2 by Robert Robinson and
stanza 3 by Robert Lowry

TAKE ME TO THE WATER
87.87 with Refrain

Take me to the wa - - - ter, take me to the
None __ but the right - eous, none __ but the

wa - ter, __ take me to the wa - ter to
right - eous. __ None __ but the right - eous __

fine ♩.=♩ In a gospel style

be bap - tized. __
shall see God. __

1. Come thou fount of eve - ry
2. O to grace how great a
3. Shall we ga - ther at the

bless - ing; tune my heart to sing thy praise. Streams of
debt - or dai - ly I'm con - strained to be. Let thy
ri - ver where bright an - gels' feet have trod. With its

arr. C. Michael Hawn

mer - cy   ne - ver   ceas - ing   call for songs of   loud - est praise.
good - ness like   a   fet - ter   bind my wan - d'ring heart to   Thee.
cry - stal   tide for - ev - er   flow - ing by   the   throne of God.

Water of life: 58
A baptismal prayer of praise

We thank you, God, for water.
    By it you give life to plants, animals and all humankind.
We thank you that in the beginning your Spirit of creation
    moved over the face of the waters.
We thank you for your rainbow covenant promise
    that emerged from the drowning flood waters.
We thank you for safe passage of our ancestors
    through the Red Sea,
    passing from slavery to freedom.
We thank you for quenching the thirst of our ancestors
    with water from the rock at Horeb.
We thank you for the baptism of Jesus
    in the waters of the River Jordan.
We thank you for Jesus who stilled raging water;
    who offered "living water,
    a spring of water welling up to eternal life,"
    who washed the disciples' feet
    to signify their continuing vocation.
We thank you, God, that you have led us by still waters.
We thank you for the promise that one day justice will flow like the waters,
    righteousness like an everflowing stream.
We thank you for creating us in the watery womb of our mothers
    and for recreating us in the watery womb of baptism,
    as we are "buried with Christ into death,
    so that as Christ was raised from the dead by the glory of God,
    we too might walk in newness of life." Amen.

Nancy Hastings Sehested

Come to me

African-American Spiritual

COME TO ME
Irregular

1. "Come to me, ye who are hard op - pressed;
2. "Come to me!" Je - ho - vah gen - tly pleads;

lay your head gen - tly up - on my breast;
"Come to me, I can sup - ply all needs;

come to me, and I will give you rest; wea - ry
and my way, un - to green pas - ture leads; free from

one, hith - er come! God is your home!"
sin! En - ter in! God is your home!"

Traditional

Who would true valor see

60

John Bunyan

1684

ST. DUNSTAN'S
65.65.6.6.6.5

1. Who would true val - or see 'gainst all di - sas - ter,
2. Who so be - set you round with dis - mal sto - ries
3. Hob - gob - lin nor foul fiend can daunt your spir - it;

come forth, and con - stant be; fol - low the Mas - ter. There's
do but them - selves con - found; your strength the more is. No
you know you at the end shall life in - her - it. Then

no dis - cour - age - ment shall make you once re - lent your
li - on can you fright, you'll with a gi - ant fight, but
fan - cies fly a - way! Fear not what oth - ers say, but

first a - vowed in - tent to be a pil - grim.
you will have the right to be a pil - grim.
la - bor night and day to be a pil - grim.

Winfred Douglas

The Savior calls

Anne Steele

1760

AZMON
CM

1. The Sav - ior calls; let eve - ry ear now hear the heav'n - ly sound. You doubt - ing souls, dis - miss your fear; hope smiles re - viv - ing round.
2. For eve - ry thirst - y, long - ing heart here streams of boun - ty flow and life and health and bliss im - part to ban - ish mor - tal woe.
3. Here springs of sa - cred plea - sures rise to ease your eve - ry pain; im - mor - tal foun - tain, full sup - plies! Nor shall you thirst in vain.
4. You sin - ners, come, 'tis mer - cy's voice; the gra - cious call o - bey; mer - cy in - vites to heav'n - ly joys, and can you yet de - lay?
5. Dear Sav - ior, draw re - luc - tant hearts; to You let sin - ners fly and take the bliss Your love im - parts and drink and nev - er die.

Carl G. Gläser; arr. Lowell Mason

I will journey

1960

Justino Quispe
translation: Janet Holmes

PACO
Irregular

Unison

1. I will jour - ney on the way with my Sav - ior
   God will guide and guard my steps; keep - ing by God's

2. Now I ask "whom shall I fear?" Guid - ed by my
   All my sor - rows borne a - way Christ came in my

3. O friend will not you de - cide now to march on
   Turn your eyes to Je - sus' cross where He bore our

ev - er near, hap - py in God's care.
won - drous love, joy to know God's there.
Sav - ior dear I shall walk se - cure.
heart to stay, re - fuge safe and sure.
Je - sus' side? Choose His lov - ing way.
sin and loss. Do not more de - lay.

Harmony

Wan - der - ing, I lost the road. Je - sus called me
Now I'll tell His love a - broad; sing I must of
He will give true hap - pi - ness, joy and peace your

where I roamed. Led me gen - tly home.
new so good, freed from sin's al - lure.
soul to bless. Come to Christ to - day.

attr. Norman K. Giesbrecht

The decision

V. Michael McKay

1992

THE DECISION
Irregular

Adagio
In a Gospel style

It's your de - ci - sion who you will live for. Will it be
cid - ed who I will live for. I chose

Je - sus or some oth - er god?
Je - sus as my Lord and King;
Since He de -
oh, He de -

cid - ed to die just to save you, it's your de - ci - sion, what will you do?
cid - ed to die just to save me, I have de - cid - ed to live for Him.

1. Oh, I've de- (Him)
2. It's a priv - i - lege to live for

V. Michael McKay

C min/Bb Bb D 7sus 4 D 9 A°/G G min C 9 F 7sus 4 F 7 F 7

Je-sus; get-ting to know Him makes my life worth-while. He fills my

C min/Bb Bb Bb/D Bb7 F min/Eb Eb G 7#5b9 C min Bb/D C min/Eb Bb/F C min C min 7 Bb/D G 7 C min

emp-ti-ness with peace and hap-pi-ness. I have de-cid-ed, have you de-

Bb/F G 7 C min 7 Bb/D C min Bb9/F Bb/F F 7sus 4 Bb7 Bb9

cid-ed? I have de-cid-ed to live for Him.

Consecrate me

64

Davita Joyce Vaughn and Joyce Marie Davis

CONSECRATE ME
4.4.8

1. Con - se - crate me, con - se - crate me,
2. Sanc - ti - fy me, sanc - ti - fy me,
3. Re-new my spir - it, re - new my spir - it, re-
4. I am will - ing, I am will - ing,

con - se - crate me to do Thy will.
sanc - ti - fy me to do Thy will.
new my spir - it to do Thy will.
I am will - ing to do Thy will.

Words and Music © Davita Joyce Vaughn and Joyce Marie Davis
Used by permission.

Devita Joyce Wesley and Joyce Marie Davis

65

Benediction

(Right side and left side facing each other)

Leader: Go from this place to love the Lord your God.

Left Side: With all your heart,
Right Side: With all your soul,
Left Side: With all your might,
Right Side: And your neighbor as yourself.

Left Side: Go forth in peace.
Right Side: Be of good courage.
Left Side: Hold fast to what is good.
Right Side: Rejoice in the power of the Holy Spirit.

Left Side: May the God who fills the hungry with good things, fill us with Christlike love,
Right Side: And with a consuming hunger for justice in our land and in your world.

All: **Amen and amen!**

Nancy Hastings Sehested

66

Benediction

Men: Peace to the nations, east and west.

Women: Peace to our neighbors, black and white.

Men: Peace to our friends, rich and poor.

Women: Peace to our families, brothers and sisters.

Men: Peace to all women;

Women: Peace to all men.

All: The peace of Christ within all peace.

Leader: Go, then, in peace.

All: **Amen.**

Mary Ruth Crook

A benediction for brothers and sisters gathered together

May the God of Abraham call your name into the journey of promise.

May the God of Hagar bring you comfort in the desert of desolation.

May the God of Deborah grant you wisdom and courage for every battle.

May the God of Jeremiah write an everlasting covenant upon your heart.

May the Christ of Simon Peter strengthen your faith
    and make steadfast your witness.

**May the Christ who met the Samaritan woman
    lead you to the spring of water always welling up.**

May the Christ who healed the blind man
    and the bleeding woman heal your pain.

**All:
In the name of Jesus the Christ
    who is the memory, hope, and authority of all of our futures.
Amen.**

Mary Zimmer

© 1994 Mary Zimmer. Used by permission.

Benediction

Leader: Now let your servants, Almighty Master,
             Slip quietly away in peace, as you've said.

**People: For these eyes of ours have seen your deliverance
             Which you have made possible for all of the people.**

Leader: It's a light to illuminate the problem of races,

All: A light to bring honor to your faithful disciples. Amen.

Clarence Jordan

Clarence Jordan, paraphrase of "Song of Simeon" and Luke 2, in The Cotton Patch Version of Luke and Acts: Jesus' Doings and the Happenings (New York, NY: Associated Press, 1968). Used by permission.

69

Blest be the tie that binds

John Fawcett

BOYLSTON
SM

1. Blest be the tie that binds our hearts in Christ - ian love;
2. Be - fore our Fa - ther's throne we pour our ar - dent prayers;
3. We share our mu - tual woes; our mu - tual bur - dens bear;
4. When we a - sun - der part, it gives us in - ward pain;
5. This glor - ious hope re - vives our cour - age by the way;
6. From sor - row, toil and pain, and sin, we shall be free;

the fel - low - ship of kin - dred minds is like to that a - bove.
our fears, our hopes, our aims are one, our com - forts and our cares.
and of - ten for each o - ther flows the sym - pa - thiz - ing tear.
but we shall still be joined in heart, and hope to meet a - gain.
while each in ex - pect - ta - tion lives, and longs to see the day.
and per - fect love and friend-ship reign through all e - ter - ni - ty.

Lowell Mason
Alternate tune: DENNIS

Litany for the Pilgrim

Leader: Where do you go from us, Pilgrim?

Pilgrim(s): We go to establish a new place for ourselves.
We go to establish new work, new schools, new friendships,
and new opportunities for faith.
We go to enter the fellowship of a new church.

People: What do you desire from us, Pilgrim?

Pilgrim(s): We desire to be a part of the living memory of this place,
a part of the prayers and shared concerns expressed here.

**People: With joy, Pilgrim,
we shall remember your sojourn with us.
You have been a vital member of this community of faith.
Our prayers are with you as you journey from us
to establish a new place of service.
You shall always be bound to us by our memories,
our prayers, and our relationships
as your brothers and sisters in the family of God.**

Pilgrim(s): We, likewise, bind ourselves to you in loving memory.
We will continue to be supportive of this community of faith
through the faith we find ahead.

**All: You have bound us together in the church, O God,
and built up the spirit of love among us.
Though we must go separate ways
in working for your kingdom,
help us to know that we are joined forever
in your loving care.
We thank you for years together,
for mutual support and mutual forgiveness.
Never let friendship fade,
but keep us remembering one another
and grateful for the life we have shared
in Jesus Christ, our Lord. Amen.**

Willard Brown

71 *Forever loved, forever blessed*

C. David Matthews
1992

REMEMBRANCE
77.65 with Refrain

C. David Matthews

A litany for All Saints' Day

Based on Ecclesiastes 3:1, 2a, 4

One: For everything there is a season
     and a time for every matter under heaven.

All: **A time to be born and a time to die,**
     A time to weep and a time to laugh,
     A time to grieve and a time to dance.

One: Now is our time to remember those who have preceded us
     across the river into the land of eternal joy.

All: **A father, a mother, a sister, a brother,**
     A son, a daughter, a husband, a wife,
     A friend closer than sister or brother.

One: They were the ones who shaped us,
     who nurtured and taught and encouraged us.

All: **Who understood us as we had never been**
     understood before and seldom since.
     They stood up for us, walked beside us,
     and went all the way for us.

Lord, make us more like the good that was in them,
Wiser through their gifts to us,
Richer through their belief in us,
Stronger through their faith in us,
That as long as we live
Their good influence will live through us,
As does the redeeming power of Christ our Lord.
Amen.

E. Lee Phillips

Litany for a Holocaust remembrance

Look deep into thyself, O soul,
And ask what it is that compels,
drives,
maddens,
urges you to violence?

O the names of horrors:
Auschwitz
Buchenwald
Dachau
Treblinka.

Can man, woman, child contemplate
Anything so horrid,
So inhuman?

Some did . . .

O the names of horrors:
Kigali
Sarajevo
Phnom Penh. . .

Can man, woman, child contemplate
Anything so horrid,
So inhuman?

Some do . . .

Holocausts remembered shock our whole being.
Holocausts remembered have snatched us away
from false assurances and mistaken dreams.
Holocausts remembered have taken us from behind our backs
and made us look at ourselves.
O God, deliver us from ourselves.
Create in us a new and right spirit
that no Holocaust happen ever again. Amen.

E. Glenn Hinson

Litany for the dedication of a music ministry

Leader: We gather to dedicate our music ministry to the glory of God. The psalmist enjoins us, "Make a joyful noise unto the Lord." By placing the words of our faith to music we proclaim a biblical message. For centuries the music of the church has brought conviction, encouragement, and instruction to multitudes of believers. Through sacred music we recall the activity of God in the birth, ministry, crucifixion, resurrection, ascension, and abiding presence of Christ Jesus our Savior. We sing first in praise to God our Maker and as we do so we implore all who hear to respond to the mighty acts of God. Choir, what is your response?

Choir: We are awed by the privilege of sharing biblical truth in musical ways. Under the leadership of the Holy Spirit we will seek to voice in sacred sequences of sound the gospel message of salvation. We cannot remain silent: our voices must proclaim what our hearts affirm!

Congregation: **We dedicate ourselves to join the choir in their glad affirmation of praise to God, following where they lead. May our part always be in harmony of spirit with the choir as together "in psalms, hymns, and spiritual songs, we sing and make melody to the Lord."**

Choir and
Congregation: **Let the clear sounds of children, the changing timbre of teenagers, the mature resonance of adults, the soft sounds of the aged blend together as one great choir in exaltation to the glory of God.**

All: **This we affirm: our earthly praises will one day be transformed into heavenly praises around the throne of God. Praise to the Lord. Praise to the Lord in glad song evermore!**

E. Lee Phillips

75 *Let the children come*

G. Temp Sparkman 1983 ST. AGNES
CM

1. Chil- dren be - long where par - ents' faith in rich de - vo - tion lives;
2. Sal - va - tion plant - ed by God's grace now comes to bud, and grows
3. Je - sus said, "Let the chil - dren come; for - bid them not their place;

where con- gre - ga - tion wor - ships God, and Chris- tian nur - ture gives.
by se- cret pow - er small seeds hold till the full flow - er grows.
for in their sim - ple faith re - sides the King-dom's joy and grace."

Words © 1983 G. Temp Sparkman
Used by permission.

John B. Dykes

76 *Litany for the dedication of a child*

Minister: We are here today to present (child's name) to the church
and to dedicate her/him to God.
Who brings this child for this holy purpose?

Parents: We, her/his parents, bring (first name)
to be dedicated to God.

Minister: What can we affirm about (first name)?

**People: That she/he is made in the image of God,
and is a child of God by creation.**

Minister: As (first name) grows in our congregation,
how will we show that she/he is a child of God?

People: We will give her/him our love and will include her/him
        in the experience of the congregation.

Minister: As (first name) grows into childhood,
        what will we tell her/him about her/his history?

People: We will tell her/him about Abraham, the father of our faith;
        about Sarah, the mother of Isaac;
        about Moses, who led our ancestors out of bondage;
        about Ruth's example of faithfulness;
        about the Jewish hope for a Messiah;
        about Mary and Joseph's openness to mystery;
        about Jesus Christ the Savior;
        and about the history of the church
            as the people of God.

Minister: What will we expect of (first name)?

People: We look to the day when she/he will
        sit with us at the Lord's Table,
        declare faith in Jesus Christ,
        confirm the heritage that we pass along to her/him,
        and come as an adult to full commitment
            to God's will and work.

Minister: Do you, (first name)'s parent(s),
        assume your primary responsibility
        for keeping (first name) in touch with such expectations?

Parent(s): Yes, I/we happily and genuinely accept this serious duty.

Minister: And do you, the congregation, pledge to work toward
        creating a nurturing environment for (first name)?

People: Yes, we do, for she/he belongs to us as well.

Minister: Then may God be with us.

People: God help us.

All: **Amen.**

G. Temp Sparkman

G. Temp Sparkman, "Litany for the Dedication of a Child," in *The Salvation and Nurture of the Child: The Story of Emma* (Valley Forge, PA: Judson Press, 1983). Used by permission.

77 *My country, 'tis of thee*

Stanza 1: Samuel F. Smith
Stanzas 2-4: Ralph Lightbody and Ken Sehested

1832/1991

AMERICA
664.6664

1. My coun-try, 'tis of thee, sweet land of li - ber-ty,
2. We are a peo - ple free, join - ing in li - ber - ty
3. Guid-ing us in the past, God's hand has held us fast,
4. My coun-try, 'tis of thee, strug - gling for li - ber-ty,

of thee I sing. Land where my fa - thers died,
our ma - ny throngs. Through much di - ver - si - ty,
God's pow'r we feel. May right - eous - ness be claimed,
of thee I sing. Land where my peo - ple died,

land of the pil - grims' pride, from eve - ry
grant sol - i - dar - i - ty turn - ing from
true jus - tice be sus - tained; Spi - rit, with
bril - liant with na - ture's pride, from plain and

moun - tain - side, let free - dom ring!
en - mi - ty in joy - ful song.
us re - main, Christ's love re - veal.
moun - tain - side let free - dom ring!

Thesararus Musicus

Cristo padeció

Spanish words by Philip W. Blycker
English translation by C. Michael Hawn

1972

PADECIÓ
Irregular

Philip W. Blycker

A litany of rededication

Martin Luther King, Jr., was a preacher and prophet,
    with a dream of justice and peace for all people.
And this is what he said:

> I am convinced that if we are to get on the right side
>   of the world revolution,
>   we as a nation must undergo a radical revolution of values.
> We must rapidly begin to shift from a "thing-oriented" society
>   to a "person-oriented" society.
> When machines, computers, profit motives and property rights
>   are considered more important than people,
> the giant triplets of racism, materialism and militarism
>   are incapable of being conquered.[1]

To this dream we rededicate ourselves.

Martin Luther King, Jr., wanted to be remembered as a "drum major for justice." And this is what he said:

> There are some things in our society and in our world
>   of which I'm proud to be maladjusted,
>   which I call upon all people of good will to be maladjusted,
>   until the good society is realized.
> I never intend to become adjusted to segregation and discrimination.
> I never intend to adjust myself to economic conditions
>   that will take necessities from the many
>   to give luxuries to the few.
> I never intend to adjust myself to the madness of militarism
>   and the self-defeating effects of physical violence.[2]

To this dream we rededicate ourselves.

Martin Luther King, Jr., preached non-violence and an end to war.
    When he received the Nobel Peace Prize he said:

> I refuse to accept the cynical notion
>   that nation must spiral down a militaristic stairway
>   into the hell of thermonuclear destruction...
> Sooner or later,
>   all the people of the world will have to discover a way
>   to live together in peace...
> [We] must evolve for all human conflict a method
>   which rejects revenge, aggression and retaliation.
> The foundation of such a method is love.[3]

To this dream we rededicate ourselves.

Martin Luther King, Jr., stood against violence in any form.
     He believed passionately in the strength of love.
And this is what he said:

> *I could never again raise my voice against the violence*
> > *of the oppressed in the ghettos*
> > *without having first spoken clearly to the greatest purveyor*
> > *of violence in the world today —*
> > *my own government...*
> *The war in Vietnam is but a symptom of a far deeper malady*
> > *within the American spirit,*
> > *and if we ignore this sobering reality,*
> > *we will find ourselves organizing... for the next generation.*
> *They will be concerned about Guatemala and Peru.*
> *They will be concerned about Thailand and Cambodia.*
> *They will be concerned about Mozambique and South Africa.*
> *We will be marching for these and a dozen other names;*
> > *and attending rallies without end*
> > *unless there is a significant and profound change*
> > *in American life and policy.*[4]

To this dream we rededicate ourselves.

Martin Luther King, Jr., was killed while working for garbage workers in
Memphis. And this is what he said:

> *A nation that continues year after year*
> > *to spend more money on military defense*
> > *than on programs of social uplift*
> > *is approaching spiritual death.*[5]

**"Now let us rededicate ourselves to the long and bitter —
     and beautiful — struggle for a new world."[6] AMEN!**

Note: All citations above have been taken from *A Testament of Hope: The Essential Writings of Martin Luther King, Jr.*, James Melvin Washington, Ed. (New York: Harper & Row, 1986).

[1]from "A Time to Break Silence," p. 240
[2]from "The American Dream," p. 218
[3]from "Nobel Prize Acceptance Speech," p. 226
[4]from "A Time to Break Silence," pp. 233, 240
[5]from "A Time to Break Silence," p. 241
[6]from "A Time to Break Silence," p. 243

This litany was especially developed for the 1986 official King Week "peace and justice" service at Ebenezer Baptist Church, Atlanta, Georgia. It was edited by Rev. T. Melvin Williams (then of Oakhurst Baptist Church, Decatur, Georgia) in consultation with Rev. Emory Searcy, Jr. (Atlanta Clergy and Laity Concerned), Rev. Ken Sehested (Baptist Peace Fellowship of North America), and Rev. Albert C. Winn (retired, North Decatur Presbyterian Church). The Reverend Dr. Joseph R. Roberts, Jr., is the pastor of Ebenezer Baptist Church, Atlanta, Georgia.

80

Collect for the ordination of a minister

Candidate for Ordination:
Jesus, I your minister bow before you to confess the common sins
   of my calling.
You know all things;
      you know that I love you
      and that my heart's desire is to serve you in faithfulness;
      and yet, like Peter, I have so often failed you
      in the hour of your need.
If ever I should love my own leadership and power
      when I seek to lead your people to you,
      I pray that you will forgive me.
If I become engrossed in narrow duties and little questions,
      when the vast needs of humanity call aloud
      for prophetic vision and apostolic sympathy,
      I pray that you will forgive me.
If in my loyalty to the church of the past I distrust your living voice
      and suffer you to pass from your door unheard,
      I pray that you will forgive me.
If ever I become more concerned for the strong and the rich than for the
      shepherdless throngs of the people for whom your soul grieved,
      I pray that you will forgive me.

People's Prayer of Consecration:
O Master, amidst our failures
      we cast ourselves upon you in humility and contrition.
We need a new light and a new message.
We need the ancient spirit of prophecy
      and the leaping fire and joy of a new conviction,
      and you alone can give it.
Inspire this Church with dauntless courage
      to face the vast needs of the future.
Free us from all entanglements that have hushed our voice
      and bound our action.
Give us your inflexible sternness against sin,
      and your inexhaustible compassion
      for the frailty and tragedy of those who do the sin.

All: Make us faithful shepherds of your flock,
      true seers of God, and true followers of Jesus. Amen.

Walter Rauschenbusch

Adapted from *Prayers of the Social Awakening* by Walter Rauschenbusch (New York: The Pilgrim Press, 1910).

EPILOGUE

An Introduction to
An African-American Traditional Prayer

The following prayer is well known in the African-American church. It is a model prayer in the African oral prayer tradition in America. Today, in many Black congregations, especially Black Baptist churches, this prayer is still being prayed. In truth, the real custodian of this prayer is the African-American community. It belongs to no particular person or denomination.

This prayer is placed as an epilogue for this collection because it encompasses the general organizational structure of the volume. The contents page suggests a structure that follows a general order of worship that is found in many churches. And so it is with this prayer. It begins with salutation, moves to thanksgiving, to petition, to intercession, and to benediction. Through this prayer Black people ordered themselves in a way that set them free to be for one another, to express their most glorious hope, and to move from social limitations to a dynamic celebration of life. Coinage of novel phrases testifies to their artistic determination to create themselves anew out of the muck and mire of oppression's madness. In spite of the chaos of social injustice and oppression, they stood on the only reality they had — God and each other — and ordered themselves into an existence which affirmed that indeed they were children of God with their souls set free.

There is no hard data to document the regional source of this prayer; however, it probably has southern roots. This prayer was probably born among slaves and/or ex-slaves, and traveled with the people during periods of migration, especially from south to north. As Black Baptist and Methodist churches gathered for fellowship, worship and denominational causes, generation after generation heard and reproduced this prayer. It probably did not come into existence full-blown as we know it in the oral prayer tradition. There is no single version of this prayer; however, its form, along with some core images and phrases, remains essentially unchanged.

Thomas W. Spann

An African-American traditional prayer

Almighty God,
> it is once more and again that a few of your humble children
> come knee-bent and body-bowed before your throne of grace
> to call upon your holy name.
We come as empty pitchers before a full fountain,
> ready to be filled.
We don't come before you for any outside show, form or fashion,
> as in this unfriendly world.
We come to worship you in spirit and in truth,
> and to give to you some true and humble thanks.

We thank you that you watched over us all night
> while we slumbered and slept.
Early this morning, while we slept in the very image of death,
> you touched us with the finger of love
> and we beheld a day that we have never seen before
> and that we will never see again.
We thank you that the blood was still running warm in our veins
> and that we had a reasonable portion of health and strength.
We were able to get up clothed in our right mind.
Through your goodness and mercy you have seen fit to leave us here
> where we can pick and choose our own praying ground.
We thank you that you have allowed our golden moments
> to roll on just a little while longer.
We thank you for protecting us from dangers seen and unseen.

We come now, Lord, thanking you for your darling son Jesus,
> who hung, bled, and died on Calvary's cross.
He stayed in the grave all night Friday,
> all night Saturday,
> but early Sunday morning he got up with all power in his hands.
We thank you that because of him we have a right to the tree of life.

God, our help,
> continue to throw around us your strong arms of protection.
Strengthen us where we are weak;
> build us up where we are torn down,
> and prop us up on every leaning side.
Bind us together in one band of Christian love.
Give us that love that runs from heart to heart and from breast to breast.

Now, Lord, we ask you to search our hearts and,
  if you find anything contrary to your holy and divine will,
  just move it from us, as far as the east is from the west.
O cast it into the sea of forgetfulness where it will never rise against us.
O, Lord, you know our hearts.
You know our heart's desires.
You know when we are right and you know when we are wrong.
You know all about us because you made us and shaped us
  in your own image.

We come, O Lord, confessing that we need you
  and that we cannot get along without you.
If it had not been for you on our side, O God,
  we would have been blown by the wayside.
We need you to go with us and stand by us as we travel this tedious journey.

Now, Lord, we pray for every church door that stands open in your name.
We remember those who stand to proclaim your word
  between the living and the dead.
Your word is sharper than any two-edged sword;
  it goes down between the marrow and the bone.
O stand by them, Lord.
Strengthen them where they are weak
  and build them up where they are torn down.
Let them down in the deep treasures of your word
  so that our weary souls may be revived.

And now, Lord,
  we pray that when we are through singing and praying down here,
when we have to stack hymnbooks and Bibles
  and study war no more,
  you will welcome us into that land
   where the wicked shall cease from troubling
   and the weary shall be at rest;
  where every day will be Sunday and Sabbath will have no end.
We pray in the name of Jesus,
  our Rock in a weary land
  and our Shelter in the time of storm. Amen.

Adpt. by Thomas W. Spann. Used by permission.

Guide my feet

African-American spiritual

1. Guide my feet
2. Hold my hand
3. Stand by me
4. I'm your child
while I run this race,

(Yes, my Lord!)

5. Search my heart...
6. Guide my feet...

guide my feet
hold my hand
stand by me
I'm your child
while I run this race,

(Yes, my Lord!)

guide my feet
hold my hand
stand by me
I'm your child
while I run this race, for I

don't want to run this race in vain! (race in vain!)

harmonization by Wendall Whalum

INDEXES FOR THE HYMNS

CONTENTS

BIOGRAPHICAL INFORMATION
ON CONTRIBUTORS

Darrell E. Adams (b. 1949) was raised in New Mexico and Texas. He graduated from Oklahoma Baptist University and did graduate study at Southern Baptist Theological Seminary. Since 1978 Mr. Adams has been a singer, songwriter, and producer, performing in a wide variety of venues including radio and TV. He now resides in Louisville, Kentucky, where he is an active member of Crescent Hill Baptist Church. He has produced five albums under the label of Windmill Power Music, the latest being *Ain't This Boy a Wonder* (1994) and *What Are People For?* (1995). "Psalm 51" (30) evolved from "Let Me Start Over Again," a confessional song written in 1977 for use in worship and published in 1981 by Broadman Press in *Singing Is Fun*. Keeping the original tune, a new text based more specifically on the psalm was written in 1994 for this volume. The song is most effective when sung with guitar and as a three-part round.

Philip W. Blycker (b. 1939) was born in Oak Park, Illinois, and grew up in nearby Chicago where he was a member of Mont Clare Baptist Church. A graduate of Bob Jones University, and VanderCook College of Music, he is currently pursuing the Doctor of Musical Arts degree at Southwestern Baptist Theological Seminary in Fort Worth, Texas. Mr. Blycker was called to be a missionary when he was a member of First Baptist Church, Warren, Illinois. At that time he was a public school band director and church choir director. He served as director of the department of music at the Central American Theological Seminary in Guatemala City and the Pueblo Bible Seminary in Mexico. "Cristo padeció" ("You have suffered") (78) appeared recently in the Hispanic hymnal *Celebremos Su Gloria* (1992), of which Mr. Blycker is the musical editor. The English translation was prepared for publication in *For the Living of These Days* by the editor. The hymn reflects on Christ's suffering and is based on 1 Peter 3:18.

Mwalimu Glenn T. Boyd (b. 1935) is a Southern Baptist missionary in Kenya. A native of Oklahoma, Boyd holds music degrees from Oklahoma Baptist University and Southwestern Baptist Theological Seminary. He and his wife, Jeanine, served in Kenya 1971-1980. Reappointed in 1988, they teach at the Baptist Seminary in Limuru. From 1980 to 1988, Glenn Boyd was director of church music for the Baptist General Convention of Oklahoma. The Swahili term "mwalimu" is a designation of respect for a teacher. He wrote "Psalm 136" (7) in collaboration with Baptist seminary students in Arusha, Tanzania. Based on a traditional Kihaya tune, it uses the customary African call-response musical form.

Willard Brown (b. 1943) is a native of North Carolina. Dr. Brown graduated from Campbell College (now University), Southeastern Baptist Theological Seminary, and Emory University. Now retired, he served churches in Georgia and North Carolina for twenty-two years. He contributes the "Litany for the Pilgrim" (70). The idea for this litany of farewell came from a pastor's conference in Raleigh, North Carolina, around 1980 during which noted pastoral theologian Wayne Oates commented that congregations do not say "good-bye" very well. Dr. Brown revised the "Litany for the Pilgrim" upon finding a similar rite written by another church for a departing staff member. The "Litany for the Pilgrim" was first used at Wake Forest Baptist Church on the campus of Southeastern Seminary, Wake Forest, North Carolina.

Jack Bruce (b. c. 1959) is a mixed-race or cosmopolitan South African. He is an ordained Baptist pastor with the predominately black Baptist Convention of Southern Africa. He lives in Ennerdale, a township of Johannesburg, which was reserved for the "coloured" population in apartheid South Africa. A community activist, Rev. Bruce recently completed an inter-governmental internship in the United States sponsored by the African National Congress (ANC). His hymn "The Lord has made me with dignity" (40) reflects not only the struggle of black South Africans, but the struggle of all oppressed peoples.

John Bunyan (1628-1688) was a British Baptist preacher known best for his publication *The Pilgrim's Progress* (1684), an allegorical narrative based on the struggles and temptations of the character Christian with the forces of evil. "Who would true valor see" (60) comes from the second part of this story. Originally beginning "He who would valiant be," it was written while Bunyan was confined in the Bedford Gaol.

Leonard Busher (*fl.* 1614) was probably a member of Thomas Helwys' church in London. He wrote a tract entitled *Religious Peace or a plea for liberty of conscience* from which the quotation in the "Litany in Celebration of Religious Liberty" (36) is taken. He also advocated adult baptism by immersion thirty years before the Particular Baptists in England adopted this mode.

Lucie Eddie Campbell (1885-1963) was the most powerful and influential musical voice in the National Baptist Convention, U.S.A., Inc., as music director of the Baptist Training Union Congress from 1916-1962. A native of Mississippi, Ms. Campbell graduated from Rust College, Holly Springs, Mississippi. She taught at the Booker T. Washington High School in Memphis, Tennessee, for forty years. She chose the music and musicians, setting the tone for the annual National Baptist conventions, occasions for which she wrote most of her forty-five gospel songs, including one new song for each year between 1930 and 1962. According to Horace Clarence Boyer, "Campbell was so important and powerful in the National Baptist Convention that anyone who wanted to sing on the program had to audition for her, singing the same song he or she planned to sing on the program." Her songs have been recorded by some of the greatest gospel singers, including Mahalia Jackson. She died after moving to Nashville, Tennessee. "The Lord is my shepherd" (29) was copyrighted in 1919 and published in the important collection of gospel songs, *Gospel Pearls* (1921 edition).

J. Nathan Corbitt (b. 1950) served as an ethnomusicologist and communications specialist for Southern Baptists in Kenya and Zimbabwe between 1981 and 1992, and is currently associate professor of music and communications, Eastern College (Pennsylvania). Dr. Corbitt holds degrees in music from Mars Hill College, Southern Baptist Theological Seminary and Southwestern Baptist Theological Seminary. He is the musical arranger of two East African selections in this hymnal, "Mwamba ni Yesu" (6) and "Psalm 136" (7). These arrangements are faithful to East African musical style.

Mary Ruth Crook (b. 1922) graduated from Florida State University and Southern Baptist Theological Seminary. An active member of the Baptist Peace Fellowship of North America, she often goes on mission trips with her husband, Roger, including recent trips to Cuba, Bolivia, and the former Soviet Republic of Georgia. A member of Pullen Memorial Baptist Church in Raleigh, she is the unofficial "chaplain" of the chancel choir and offers a prayer on behalf of the choir before they sing for each service. She contributes a benediction (66).

Joyce Marie Davis (b. 1933) has been director of the Lucie E. Campbell Church Music Workshop, an event sponsored by the National Baptist Convention, U.S.A., Inc. She resides in Denver, Colorado, where she is the minister of music at Zion Baptist Church and is in constant demand for church music workshops throughout the country. Dr. Davis graduated from Prairie View University and the University of Colorado and received a Doctor of Humane Letters from Central America University. She teaches music in the Denver Public Schools and has received many honors and awards for her service to music education. She contributes "Consecrate me" (64).

Frances S. Dean (b. 1918) is a native of Texas, living in Abilene. She has published an illustrated book of dramatic monologues, *Bible Women Speak*, and collaborated with her husband, Talmage Dean, on a collection of hymns, *Sing in the Spirit*. She wrote "Liberty, that sweet word sounding" (41) in 1986 in response to a hymn contest announced by The Baptist Joint Committee for Public Affairs, commemorating the fiftieth anniversary of the Committee. This winning hymn was introduced during the Twentieth Religious Liberty Conference in Washington, D.C., in October, 1986.

Margaret Pleasant Douroux (b. 1941) holds degrees from California State College, University of Southern California, and the University of Beverly Hills. Dr. Douroux has served as an elementary school teacher and school psychologist in the Los Angeles Public Schools and as minister of music of the Greater New Bethel Baptist Church. She is widely known as a composer and performer of gospel music and conducts many workshops around the country. She is the composer of "Give me a clean heart" (28) and "If it had not been for the Lord" (13).

Paul D. Duke (b. 1953) graduated from Samford University and Southern Baptist Theological Seminary. Currently he is the pastor of Kirkwood Baptist Church in St. Louis, Missouri. Dr. Duke is co-author of two hymns in this volume, "We, O God, unite our voices" (11) with Grady Nutt in 1981, and "When sorrow floods the troubled heart" (24) with Rebecca Turner Lawson in 1989. He collaborated in the writing of "We, O God, unite our voices" while a member at Crescent Hill Baptist Church, Louisville, Kentucky, in celebration of the coming of H. Stephen Shoemaker as pastor. "When sorrow floods the troubled heart" was written at his current pastorate.

Marian Wright Edelman (b. 1939) is the founder and president of the Children's Defense Fund (CDF) in Washington, D.C., an organization devoted to advocacy for disadvantaged children. The many activities of the CDF promote public awareness and action in the areas of child health, education, child care, adolescent pregnancy prevention, youth employment, child welfare and mental health, and family support systems. A native of Bennettsville, South Carolina, Dr. Edelman graduated from Spelman College and Yale School of Law. Dr. Edelman lives in Washington, D.C., with her husband, Peter Edelman, a dean at Georgetown University's law school, and is a member at Shiloh Baptist Church, a congregation affiliated with the Progressive Baptist National Convention and the American Baptist Churches. She contributes "A Litany: O God of all the children" (27).

John Fawcett (1739/40-1817) was influenced by the preaching of the great English evangelist George Whitefield when only 16 years of age. In 1758 he became a Baptist, serving several smaller churches and refusing to move to larger and more prestigious parishes. While at Hebden Bridge, he used part of his home as a school for children in the neighborhood. He was also known for his early support of the new Baptist Missionary Society. "Blest be the tie that binds" (69) is said to have been written to commemorate his decision not to leave the small church at Wainsgate in 1772 for a large London parish. This song has long been a favorite of Baptists. Since most current hymnals include only four stanzas, all six of the original stanzas have been published here. While many may choose to sing this text to the familiar tune DENNIS, the editor has paired the text with the tune BOYSTON by nineteenth-century American music educator Lowell Mason as an alternative.

Kathy Manis Findley (b. 1949) has been the pastor of Providence Baptist Church of Little Rock (Arkansas) since 1992. She holds degrees from the University of Alabama and Southern Baptist Theological Seminary. Other activities include mission service to Uganda, 1980-1982, and offices in Southern Baptist Women in Ministry. Rev. Findley contributes the "Congregational Prayer of Confession" (31).

Harry Emerson Fosdick (1878-1969) is known for his many books and radio sermons and was one of the most recognized Baptist ministers of his day. He wrote three hymns at his summer home in Boothbay Harbor, Maine, in 1930. "God of grace and God of glory" (1) was one of these. It was written as the processional hymn for the opening service of the Riverside Church in New York City, October 5, 1930, and was sung again at the church's service of dedication, February 8, 1931. "O God, in restless living" (23) was written in 1931. Like the better known "God of grace," it reflects its author's hope that Christians should remain open to the power of the Holy Spirit. In addition to these two hymns, three short prayers (3, 9, 12) by Fosdick are also included.

C. Michael Hawn (b. 1948) has been a professor of sacred music at Perkins School of Theology, Southern Methodist University, since 1992. He received degrees from Wheaton College (Illinois) and Southern Baptist Theological Seminary. Before coming to SMU, he taught church music for fifteen years at two Southern Baptist seminaries and served four Baptist churches as minister of music. In addition to providing musical arrangements of "Take me to the water" (57), "The Lord has made me with dignity" (40), the English versification of "Psalm 136" (7), and the English translation of "Cristo padeció" (78), Dr. Hawn is the general editor of this volume.

Peggy Haymes (b. 1960) is an ordained Southern Baptist minister. A graduate of Furman University and Southeastern Baptist Theological Seminary, Rev. Haymes is a free-lance writer and serves as an editor of *Reflections*, a daily devotional magazine published by Smyth & Helwys Publishers. She also also wrote a book entitled *Be Thou Present: Prayers, Litanies, and Hymns for Christian Worship* (Smyth & Helwys, 1994). Rev. Haymes served on the task force for the preparation of this hymnal and as its literary consultant. She contributes "Christ, our liberty" (33), which was written in 1993 for the annual convocation of the Cooperative Baptist Fellowship in Birmingham, Alabama.

Thomas Helwys (d. 1615) was pastor of the first General Baptist congregation in England. He spent the last three years of his life in prison because of his outspoken advocacy of religious liberty. He is best known for his treatise *A Short Declaration on the Mistery of Iniquity* from which the quotation in "Litany in Celebration of Religious Liberty" (36) is taken.

E. Glenn Hinson (b. 1931) graduated from Southern Baptist Theological Seminary and Oxford University. A native of Missouri, he is the author of many books about Christian spirituality, including *Seekers After Mature Faith* and *A Serious Call to a Contemplative Lifestyle*. He served for many years as professor of church history at Southern Seminary and now holds the John Loftis Chair of Church History at the Baptist Theological Seminary at Richmond. He contributes the "Litany for a Holocaust Remembrance" (73).

William Hornbuckle (b. 1939) graduated from Samford University and Southern Baptist Theological Seminary and is a member of the Board of the Alliance of Baptists. Rev. Hornbuckle wrote "O Lord, who gave us freedom's theme" (35) in 1986 and revised it in 1993 while minister of music at Highland Park Baptist Church in Austin, Texas. It is based on John 8:32 and Micah 6:8.

Donald P. Hustad (b. 1918) is a former musician for Billy Graham's crusades, a former professor at Moody Bible Institute, and an emeritus professor of church music at Southern Baptist Theological Seminary, Louisville, Kentucky. Dr. Hustad has been one of the leading spokespersons for church music in the evangelical tradition during the last half of the twentieth century. He was the musical arranger of the tune MORNING TRUMPET from *The Sacred Harp* (1844) for the text attributed to John Leland entitled "O, when shall I see Jesus" (17). This selection came from the hymnal *The Worshiping Church* (1990), edited by Dr. Hustad.

Thomas A. Jackson (b. 1931) has been the pastor of Wake Forest Baptist Church, Wake Forest, North Carolina, since 1988. He holds degrees from Towson State University, the University of Richmond, Southeastern Baptist Theological Seminary, and Johns Hopkins University. His hymn "Jacob wrestling" (45) is based on Genesis 32:22-32 and was written in 1991 after he heard Dr. Bill Leonard speak on this text to a gathering of

Friends of Missions prior to the North Carolina Baptist State Convention in Asheville. Dr. Jackson is also known for his hymn "We are called to be God's people," which appears in two Southern Baptist hymnals.

L.D. Johnson (1917-1981) received degrees from George Washington University and Southern Baptist Theological Seminary. A Southern Baptist minister, he served as the pastor of First Baptist Church, Danville, Virginia, and First Baptist Church, Greenville, South Carolina. He also served as chair of the department of religion of the University of Richmond. For the last fourteen years of his life, Dr. Johnson served as chaplain and professor of religion at Furman University. A noted speaker, he was the author of six books, the writer of a weekly newspaper column, and, for many, embodied ministry based on justice and compassion. He was once described as having "the voice of a prophet and the heart of a pastor." The litany "The Peaceable Kingdom" (39) has been adapted for this volume from his book *Images of Eternity*.

Stephen D. Jones (b. 1948) is an American Baptist pastor currently serving First Baptist Church, Birmingham, Michigan. He received degrees from William Jewell College, Colgate Rochester Divinity School, and United Theological Seminary. "We love your world, O God" (18) grows out of Dr. Jones' commitment to global/local partnerships as "the call of the church today" and is the result of extensive travel to Kenya, El Salvador, Nicaragua, the Philippines, and South Africa. The hymn was written upon the dedication of the Global Mission Residence at Central Baptist Church, Wayne, Pennsylvania, an apartment for use "by persons from the Third World (missionaries or nationals) coming to the Philadelphia area for reverse mission, education, relaxation, and consultation."

Clarence Jordan (1912-1969) was the founder of Koinonia Farm in Americus, Georgia, a pioneering interracial farming community. He was educated at the University of Georgia in agriculture and held two degrees from Southern Baptist Theological Seminary, including a Ph.D. in New Testament Greek. All of these experiences were combined to produce his famous "Cotton Patch Version" of the New Testament. A benediction (68) has been adapted from Jordan's paraphrase of the Song of Simeon in Luke 2.

Adoniram Judson (1788-1850) was the first Baptist missionary from the United States, serving in Burma. Educated at Rhode Island College (now Brown University) and Andover Newton Seminary, he initially left for India in 1812 as a Congregational minister. He was traveling with his first wife, Ann Hasseltine, when they became convinced through the reading of scripture of the Baptist view of baptism. Upon arrival in Calcutta, he was baptized by an English Baptist missionary, William Ward. In 1813 he was forced to leave India and went to Burma where the translation of the Bible into Burmese was one of many significant accomplishments during his long ministry. Judson's metrical version of The Lord's Prayer, "Our Father God, who art in heaven" (19), stays quite close to the traditional King James Version and appeared in several nineteenth-century Baptist hymnals. It was written in 1825 while Judson was imprisoned in Ava during struggles between the Burmese and British governments. Judson was buried at sea in 1850.

Martin Luther King, Jr., (1929-1968) is renowned as a civil rights leader who left a legacy for justice through nonviolent action. A graduate of Morehouse College, Atlanta, Georgia, Crozer Theological Seminary, Pennsylvania, and Boston University, Dr. King settled in Montgomery, Alabama, as pastor of Dexter Avenue Baptist Church with his wife Coretta. Soon after his arrival, he was asked to lead a boycott of the city buses. The boycott lasted 381 days and was successful when the U.S. Supreme Court declared the segregation of buses to be in violation of the Constitution in 1956. Rev. King then became president of the Southern Christian Leadership Conference (SCLC). In 1959 he returned to Atlanta, the place of his birth, as co-pastor of the Ebenezer Baptist Church with his father. The activities of the SCLC helped to bring about the Civil Rights Act of 1964 and the Voting Rights Act of 1965. The Nobel peace prize was awarded to Dr. King in 1964 for his pursuit of justice through nonviolence. Dr. Martin Luther King, Jr., was assassinated on April 4, 1968, while helping sanitation workers win better wages and working conditions. "A Litany of Rededication" (79), adapted from his writings by Ken Sehested, has been included.

Rebecca Turner Lawson (b. 1957) is serving in interim ministry in the United Church of Christ. Currently living in St. Louis, she graduated from New Orleans Baptist Theological Seminary and is a candidate for the Doctor of Ministry degree at Eden Theological Seminary. She is co-author of the hymn "When sorrow floods the troubled heart" (24) with Paul Duke. This hymn was written in response to a sermon preached by Dr. Duke at the first Convocation of the Southern Baptist Alliance (now Alliance of Baptists) in 1987 and as a result of shared grief over Southern Baptist refusal to accept the ministry gifts of women. It recalls a Hasidic saying often quoted by Abraham Heschel: "There are three ascending levels of how one mourns: with tears . . . with silence . . . and with song."

John Leland (1754-1841) was born in Massachusetts, but became well-known as a Virginia Baptist preacher who was said to have delivered over 8,000 sermons. He wrote many hymns. The hymn "O, when shall I see Jesus" (17) reflects the eschatological fervor of camp meeting songs. Although the hymn is attributed to Leland and reflects his style, there is some doubt that Leland actually wrote this hymn. The hymn was a part of the revivals that swept the southeastern United States during the first half of the nineteenth century in what Walter Shurden calls the "Sandy Creek Tradition." Leland is also quoted in "The Litany in Celebration of Religious Liberty" (36).

Ralph Lightbody (b. 1926) was born in Boston and educated at Gordon College, Andover Newton Theological School, and San Francisco Theological Seminary. He has served American Baptist pastorates on both coasts and is now retired, living in Claremont, California. His new stanzas to "My country, 'tis of thee" (77) were used in worship at the biennial meeting of the American Baptist Churches in June, 1991. Ken Sehested further modified the stanzas that are included in the hymnal.

W. Randall Lolley (b. 1931) is pastor of First Baptist Church, Greensboro, North Carolina. He was the third president of Southeastern Baptist Theological Seminary, Wake Forest, North Carolina, from 1974 until 1988. In the wake of the takeover of the Board of Trustees of the seminary by a fundamentalist faction in October, 1987, he wrote an additional stanza ("Addendum") to the six original stanzas of the Southeastern Seminary hymn, "Ordained of God, his prophets rise," [changed to "true prophets" for this volume] (46) with fellow alumnus Robert Mullinex. Changes in the membership and philosophy of the Board of Trustees set the stage for his resignation as seminary president. The stanza beginning "For freedom Christ has set us free" is a reaction to the narrow interpretation of scripture imposed upon the faculty and students by the new majority of fundamentalist trustees and is the only substantial change to the original hymn penned by Edward A. McDowell, Jr., in 1954.

Patricia V. Long (b. 1951) is a member of Pullen Memorial Baptist Church, Raleigh, North Carolina, where she sings in the choir and serves as a deacon. A native of Virginia and an accountant by profession, Ms. Long graduated from Eckerd College in St. Petersburg, Florida, and has also pursued theological study on the seminary level. She is active in justice issues in the Raleigh area, working with the homeless for many years. She contributes often to the liturgical life of Pullen Church. A poet since seven years of age, Ms. Long wrote both the text and music of "Beloved God" (5) in honor of the church's pastor M. Mahan Siler in 1989.

Robert Lowry (1826-1899) was a popular Baptist preacher, speaker, and educator, pastoring churches in the northeast United States. He was the writer of many gospel songs and the compiler of many collections. The text of "How can I keep from singing" (22) is well known in its Quaker version. The text printed here comes from Lowry's collection *Bright Jewels for the Sunday School* (1869), although it may have been sung much earlier. Lowry is indicated as the composer, but there is no indication of the author. The first stanza of Lowry's "Shall we gather at the river" (57), written in 1864 in Brooklyn, New York, has been used with the African-American baptismal spiritual "Take me to the water." While it is technically a funeral hymn based on Revelations 22:1-5, its use of water imagery makes the first stanza appropriate for use within the context of baptism.

C. David Matthews (b. 1940) was born in Texas where he graduated from Baylor University and Southwestern Baptist Theological Seminary. He has served as pastor in several Southern Baptist congregations and is currently the pastor of Good Samaritan Church in Orlando, Florida, where he has been since the founding of the congregation in 1987. Concerning the hymn "Forever loved, forever blessed" (71), Dr. Matthews stated in a letter to the editor, "I wrote it in 1992 simply out of frustration that 'For All the Saints,' one of my favorite hymns, was about all we had for All Saints' Sunday."

Thomas B. McDormand (1904-1988) was a beloved Canadian Baptist leader. Born in Bear River, Nova Scotia, he served Canadian Baptists from coast to coast. He began his studies for ministry at Acadia University, graduating from St. Stephen's College in Edmonton, and Victoria University in Toronto. After serving churches and the denomination in various capacities, he became General Secretary and later president of the Baptist Federation of Canada, president of Eastern Baptist Theological Seminary and Eastern Baptist College, and vice-president of the Baptist World Alliance. Of his many hymns, "From every race, from every clime" (55) is one of the favorites of Canadian Baptists, appearing in *The Hymnal* (1973). Dr. McDormand gives the following account of the writing of this hymn: "This was written for World Communion Sunday. I felt that there was no communion hymn specifically focused on the worldwide fellowship of Christians—hence this hymn. This hymn has also been used in the new hymn books of the American and Southern Baptist Conventions [*The Baptist Hymnal*, 1975]."

Edward A. McDowell, Jr. (1898-1975) was professor of New Testament Interpretation at Southeastern Baptist Theological Seminary, Wake Forest, North Carolina, from 1952 to 1964. He wrote "Ordained of God, true prophets rise" [originally "his prophets"] (46) for the first commencement of Southeastern Seminary in 1954. It has been the official hymn of the seminary since that time. The hymn remained in its original form until 1985 when minor changes were made by the faculty for the purpose of inclusive language. A seventh stanza was added to the original six in 1987 by alumni W. Randall Lolley and Robert Mullinex. Three of McDowell's stanzas appear in this volume.

William N. McElrath (b. 1932) has been a Southern Baptist missionary to Indonesia since 1965. Born in Kentucky and educated at Murray State University and Southern Baptist Theological Seminary, he has written more than 60 books in two languages, as well as hymns, songs, musical dramas, and hundreds of articles, stories, and curriculum materials. Rev. McElrath provided the translation of "Only you, O Lord my God" (25) from the original text written by Andreas Sudarsono in 1977. An author and hymn writer, Rev. McElrath prepared the English translation and simple accompaniment for inclusion in his book *Sing His Song Around the World* (1979).

V. Michael McKay (b. 1952) is a writer, composer, and conductor of music who resides in Houston, Texas. He has served as a minister of music for over twenty years and is presently musician-in-residence at Brookhollow Baptist Church in Houston where he leads worship each Sunday. Mr. McKay has an educational background in music and social work, having studied at Southern University and Texas Southern University. His many honors in composition include two Dove awards (1991 and 1992) for the Traditional Black Gospel Song of the Year and the 1993 SESAC Top Song Writer of the Year Award. Three selections are included: "The decision" (63), a song of invitation based on II Timothy 2:22 and II Peter 3:18; "In this place" (10), an invitation to worship based on Matthew 21:13a, 14-16; and "The redeemed praise" (8), a song of gratitude for redemption. In discussions with the editor, McKay stressed the importance of combining a biblically based text with a contemporary musical idiom that encourages the congregation to fully participate in music throughout the service.

Ken Medema (b. 1943) is a popular Christian concert artist known for his innovative spirit and improvisatory abilities. He received his bachelors and masters degrees from Michigan State University in the area of music therapy. Blind from birth, Mr. Medema has dedicated himself to full-time composition and concertizing since January 1, 1973, appearing around the world, including Australia, Africa, Europe and North America. Devoted to pursuing issues of peace and justice, the Medema family are members of Dolores Street Baptist Church in San Francisco. "In unity we lift our song" (4) was written for a Southern Baptist Women in Ministry conference that met at Wilshire Baptist Church in Dallas on June 8, 1985, and was premiered by Medema at this event. The hymn was also sung at the first meeting of the Alliance of Baptists (then the Southern Baptist Alliance) in Raleigh, North Carolina, in March, 1987. The four stanzas are set to the familiar Reformation melody by Martin Luther, EIN' FESTE BURG.

Samuel H. Miller (1900-1968) was pastor of Old Cambridge Baptist Church in Cambridge, Massachusetts, adjunct professor of philosophy of religion at Andover-Newton Theological School, and lecturer in pastoral theology at Harvard Divinity School. Known for his publications, including prayers, he has two "Collects for Worship" (16, 20) included from his *Prayers for Daily Use*.

T. Robert Mullinex (b. 1931) collaborated with W. Randall Lolley in writing an "Addendum" to the Southeastern Baptist Theological Seminary hymn, "Ordained of God, true prophets rise" (46) in 1987. Rev. Mullinex is an alumnus of Southeastern Seminary and works for the North Carolina State Baptist Convention as Executive Director, Council on Christian Higher Education. *See* notes on W. Randall Lolley and Edward A. McDowell, Jr., for further information.

Manaseh G. Mutsoli (b. 1937) is a pastor in the Nandi District of Kenya. Born in the Kakamega District of Kenya, he was educated in Kenya. Although he has no formal musical training, his parents were singers and encouraged him to sing and learn the music of the Luhya people and the other tribes around him. Rev. Mutsoli taught many years in the regular primary schools. In 1982 he assumed the post of music instructor jointly with the Baptist Convention and the Baptist Mission of Kenya. While in that position he composed Christian songs, among which was the contextualizing of traditional African tunes with Christian texts. "Mwamba ni Yesu" (6), found in this collection, is a text by Mutsoli with a tune of possible Luhya origin. J. Nathan Corbitt edited a book of songs entitled *Tumsifu Mungu: Songs by M. G. Mutsoli and Popular Choruses of Kenya* (1982) in which this hymn appears.

Grady Nutt (1934-1982) was a native of Texas, a graduate of Baylor University and Southern Baptist Theological Seminary, and a long-time member of Crescent Hill Baptist Church in Louisville. Rev. Nutt was best known through personal and televised appearances, recordings, and publications as a Christian humorist. He co-authored the hymn "We, O God, unite our voices" (11) in 1981 with Paul Duke in celebration of the coming of H. Stephen Shoemaker to be pastor of Crescent Hill.

E. Lee Phillips (b. 1941) is a native of Missouri who received degrees from Southwest Baptist University, Howard Payne University, Southwestern Baptist Theological Seminary, and Vanderbilt Divinity School. A resident of Atlanta, Dr. Phillips is the author of several daily worship and prayer books and has had his prayers published in *Guideposts, Decision, These Days,* and other magazines. He is a frequent pulpit guest, seminar leader, and lecturer. He contributes a "Litany for the Dedication of a Music Ministry" (74), which draws from Psalm 100, Ephesians 5:19, Isaiah 55:11, Hebrews 13:15 and Psalm 148, and "A Litany for All Saints' Day" (72) based upon Ecclesiastes 3:1, 2a, 4.

Harold E. Pinkston, Sr., (b. 1931) has earned degrees from Virginia Union University, Virginia Union School of Theology, Wesleyan University, Temple University, and Trinity Theological Seminary. Currently he is professor of English at Ohio Wesleyan University. He has served as the founding pastor of the Good Shepherd Baptist Church in Columbus since 1976. In addition to his many other honors and areas of service, he was president of the Midwest Region of the Progressive National Baptist Convention, Inc., (PNBC) from 1983-1985. Dr. Pinkston wrote the text of "Arise! Servants of Christ, arise!" (47) for the 25th anniversary of the PNBC at its annual meeting in Cincinnati, Ohio, August 4-10, 1986. The hymn was commissioned in 1984 by Charles W. Butler, former president of the PNBC, and adopted in 1985 by the Executive Committee of the PNBC, Marshall L. Shepherd, president, for presentation at the 1986 silver anniversary convention as the official hymn-anthem of the PNBC. Based on Ephesians 6:10-20 and Romans 16:27, the hymn draws from the "Progressive Concept": Fellowship, Progress, Peace, Service – words that the author has requested be italicized when they appear in the hymn.

Edwin McNeill Poteat (1892-1955) was pastor of Pullen Memorial Baptist Church in Raleigh, North Carolina, on two occasions. Before coming to Pullen, he served as a missionary to China. Between his two terms as pastor of Pullen, he was president of Colgate Rochester Divinity School in Rochester, New York. The text of "Eternal God whose searching eye doth scan" (42) was probably written in the late 1940's for the tune OIKOUMENIKOS, which Poteat had composed for an earlier hymn dated in 1930. "Eternal God" was one of nearly 500 hymns submitted for a competition at the Second Assembly of the World Council of Churches, meeting in Evanston, Illinois, in 1954. "Hope of the world," a hymn by Methodist theologian Georgia Harkness, won the competition.

Milburn Price (b. 1938) is a native of Mississippi. He earned degrees in music from the University of Mississippi, Baylor University, and the University of Southern California. He has held administrative posts at Furman University and Southern Baptist Theological Seminary, and has been dean of the School of Music at Samford University, Birmingham, Alabama, since 1993. A noted composer and conductor, he is also the co-author of *A Survey of Christian Hymnody* (3rd ed., 1987) with William J. Reynolds and has published hymns in several hymnals. "In ancient times the people yearned" (38) appears for the first time in this volume and, in the author's own words, was "written out of my own reflections and meditation during Advent of 1989. . . . The purpose of the text is to combine into one hymn the two aspects of Christ's coming that are present in the observance of Advent – the initial coming of Christ into the world as Jesus of Nazareth and his ultimate return." Dr. Price draws heavily on biblical images found in Isaiah 9:2, Isaiah 60:2, and John 1:4,9 in stanza one. Stanza two is based on Isaiah 61:1-2, and stanza three alludes to Acts 1:11.

Justino Quispe (1926-1971) was born at Huatajata, the Canadian Baptist Mission Farm on the shores of Lake Titicaca, Bolivia. He attended the mission school in Huatajata, one of the few rural schools in the country at that time. After further study in the city of Oruro, he felt called at the age of 24 to be a Baptist pastor to his native Aymara people. During study at the Cochabamba Baptist Seminary, he began a translation of Paul's Epistles into his native dialect. He served two churches in the area of La Paz, one with services in Aymara and the other in Spanish. Rev. Quispe also had a strong interest in music, playing many instruments. His favorite was the piano-accordion because of its portability. Canadian Baptists still recall fondly his visit to Canada in 1969 when he attended the General Ontario and Quebec Convention. He was especially remembered for his singing, accompanied by his accordion. "I will journey" (62) was written in both Aymara and Spanish around 1960. Through this hymn, a generation of Canadian Baptists learned of the faith and ministry of "Paco of the high country," the affectionate name for Quispe. He died prematurely of lung cancer at the age of 44.

Walter Rauschenbusch (1861-1918) was ordained to the Baptist ministry following his graduation from Rochester Theological Seminary in 1886. The son of German immigrants, he took a modest parish among the people of German descent in New York City, studying how to help meet the needs of these and others in a similar socio-economic strata. The depression of 1893 increased his awareness of suffering among the poor and prompted him to become a leading protagonist of the Social Gospel and to write many books in the area. Rauschenbusch taught New Testament and Church History at the Rochester Theological Seminary from 1897 until his death in 1918. His contributions to this volume are adapted from his *Prayers for the Social Awakening* (1910). They include "Prayer Against War" (32) and "Collect for the Ordination of a Minister" (80).

Paul A. Richardson (b. 1951) holds degrees in church music from Mars Hill College and Southern Baptist Theological Seminary. Dr. Richardson is the current president of the Hymn Society in the United States and Canada and lives in Louisville, where he teaches at Southern Baptist Theological Seminary. Beginning in the fall of 1995, Dr. Richardson will assume the post of associate dean of the music school of Samford University, Birmingham, Alabama. He contributes the Maundy Thursday hymn "As He gathered at His table" (54), which he wrote in 1986 for a hymn competition sponsored by the Southern Baptist Sunday School Board. Although the hymn did not win the contest, it appears in two recent hymnals, *The Worshiping Church* (1990) and *The Baptist Hymnal* (1991).

Robert Robinson (1735-1790) was a British Baptist who began as a barber's apprentice but fell under the spell of the great preacher George Whitefield. Following his conversion, he began preaching in the Calvinist Methodist Chapel, Mildenhall, Suffolk. He was rebaptized as a Baptist in 1759 and was the pastor of Yard Baptist Church, Cambridge, from 1761-1790. Portions of his famous hymn "Come, thou fount of every blessing" (1758) are used in the African-American baptismal spiritual "Take me to the water" (57). This text was combined with the spiritual in the *Baptist Standard Hymnal* (1961), a collection of the National Baptist Convention, U.S.A., Inc., as arranged by A.M. Townsend.

Lyn Seils Robertson (b. 1948) is chair of the Education Department at Denison University. A graduate of Denison, Northwestern, and Ohio State universities, Dr. Robertson is a member of the Feminist Sunday School Class at the First Baptist Church of Granville, Ohio (American Baptist Churches), a discussion class on spirituality and women begun in 1986. It was out of the ferment of this class that she wrote her interpretation of The Lord's Prayer that is included in this hymnal, entitled "A Traditional Prayer in a Different Voice" (21).

Jean M. Michael Sebring (b. 1955) is a native of southeastern Ohio. Ms. Sebring graduated *cum laude* with a Masters of Music in composition from Ohio University. She served as organist of the Good Shepherd Baptist Church in Columbus with Dr. Harold E. Pinkston, Sr., for four years and now resides with her family in Naples, Florida, where she is music director of Golden Gate Presbyterian Church. Ms. Sebring collaborated with Dr. Pinkston in the writing of the music for the hymn "Arise! Servants of Christ, arise" (47) for the silver anniversary of the Progressive National Baptist Convention, Inc., (PNBC) in Cincinnati, Ohio, August 4-10, 1986. She composed a hymn-anthem version of the music that was presented as the official hymn of the PNBC. The tune name PROGRESSIVE BAPTIST CHORAL was chosen by Dr. Pinkston and Ms. Sebring for this volume.

Ken Sehested (b. 1951) has been the executive director of the Baptist Peace Fellowship of North America (BPFNA) since 1984. The BPFNA is an organization of Baptists from many conventions that is devoted to furthering issues of peace and justice both in North America and around the world. A native of Oklahoma and a graduate of the City College of New York and Union Theological Seminary, Sehested was one of the co-founders of *Seeds* magazine. He collaborated with Ralph Lightbody in the writing of additional stanzas to Samuel Smith's "My country, 'tis of thee" (77), a hymn that is sung traditionally at the annual summer conferences of the BPFNA. Sehested offers these additional stanzas in the spirit of clarifying the distinction within the Baptist heritage of "allegiance to God and loyalty to one's native land." Rev. Sehested also compiled and documented "A Litany of Reconciliation" (80) from the writings of Martin Luther King, Jr.

Nancy Hastings Sehested (b. 1951) received degrees from the City College of New York and Union Theological Seminary. A native of Texas, she was ordained by Oakhurst Baptist Church, Decatur, Georgia, and currently serves as pastor of Prescott Memorial Baptist Church, Memphis, Tennessee. She is a frequent guest preacher in churches and universities as well as a contributor to periodicals. Union Theological Seminary honored Rev. Sehested with a special alumna recognition in 1994 for outstanding service in ministry. Rev. Sehested contributes "Water of Life: A baptismal prayer of praise" (58) and a benediction (65).

João Fernandes da Silva Neto (1946-1990) was born in one of the Northeastern states of Brazil (Maranhão). His pre-seminary instruction was influenced by the ministry of Conservative Baptist missionaries. João received his Bachelor of Theology degree at the North Baptist Theological Seminary in Recife, and his first music degree from the South Brazil Seminary in Rio de Janeiro. Later he received a Master of Church Music degree from Golden Gate Baptist Theological Seminary. After returning to Brazil he taught for several years at the Baptist Seminary in Curitiba, Paraná, and was minister of music of the Bacacheri Baptist Church. João is the Brazilian author of the hymn "Nestes tempos de incerteza" written in 1987. It appears in this hymnal as "In these dark, uncertain moments" (26), as translated by Joan R. Sutton in 1994. The editor needed a fresh hymn on the theme of the home and family and requested that Ms. Sutton provide a singing translation in English, based upon the original Portuguese. This hymn was originally published in the most recent Brazilian Baptist hymnal, *Hinário Para o Culto Cristão*, in 1991. The author was also the composer of the tune ECOLOGIA. João died during the final preparations for the hymnal.

Anne Skinner (b. 1916) is a Canadian Baptist, born in Hamilton, but living in Ottawa since 1940. She worked as a public servant until her retirement in 1974. She has been active in all phases of the educational life of First Baptist Church, Ottawa, and has served the Ottawa Baptist Association in several capacities including terms as director of Mission Circles, president of the Ottawa Baptist Women's Association and, finally, moderator of the Association. Ms. Skinner gives this account of her writing of "Ye people of the north," (52) one of the favorite hymns of Canadian Baptists: "One Saturday morning late in January 1967, I had planned to go to Tucker House [a Baptist retreat center] to be part of a work party. A heavy snowstorm made the 25-mile trip inadvisable, and the work party was canceled. Finding myself housebound, I decided to try my hand at writing the words of a hymn for the [Baptist] Federation [of Canada] Centennial Hymn-writing contest." She sent the text to her brother-in-law, Jack L. Hodd, who set it to a vigorous tune. The hymn was runner-up in the contest sponsored by the Baptist Federation of Canada. This popular Canadian hymn draws its stanzas from the various regions of the country.

L.J. Egerton Smith (1879-1958) received his education at Spurgeon's College and served several Baptist parishes in England. The position he held longest was that of associate minister of Silver Street Baptist Church, Taunton, from 1935 until his death. A lecturer for the Y.M.C.A. to the Armed Forces during World War II, he was among the last to leave France in 1940 in the wake of the Nazi invasion of that country. He contributes the hymn "For all the love that from our earliest days" (2) to this collection. "For all the love" reflects Smith's strong interest in education. It has been well known among British Baptists since its first appearance in the *Baptist Church Hymnal* (1933) and was chosen for the most recent British Baptist hymnal, *Baptist Praise and Worship* (1991).

Samuel Francis Smith (1808-1895) was educated at Harvard and Andover Theological Seminary. He served as a Baptist pastor in the Northeast and was secretary of the American Baptist Missionary Union for 15 years. Smith is the author of the original version of "My country, 'tis of thee" (77), which was first sung in 1931 during Independence Day exercises of the Boston Sabbath School Union, Park Street Church.

John Smyth (d. 1612) was an early English Baptist who became pastor of a Separatist congregation in Gainsborough about 1606. The intolerance and harsh policies of James I forced Smyth and his congregation into exile for their beliefs. While in Amsterdam they were influenced by the Dutch Anabaptists (Mennonites). Smyth received education from the Church of England at Cambridge, and was a student of Francis Johnson at Christ's College. Smyth is recognized by some as the "founder of the modern Baptist churches," because of his adoption of believers' baptism in his historic Confession of twenty articles written in Amsterdam in 1609. Smyth is quoted in the "Litany in Celebration of Religious Liberty" (36), compiled by Reid Trulson.

Thomas W. Spann (b. 1953) was raised in Marshall, Texas. He grew up in nearby Pine Bluff Baptist Church. He holds degrees from Bishop College, Princeton Theological Seminary, and Perkins School of Theology, Southern Methodist University. An ordained minister in the National Baptist Convention, U.S.A., Inc., Dr. Spann has taught at Shorter College (North Little Rock, Arkansas) and Jarvis Christian College (Hawkins, Texas). He is currently the associate director of the Intern Program at Perkins School of Theology, Southern Methodist University. He contributes "An African American Traditional Prayer" (81).

G. Temp Sparkman (b. 1932) is a Baptist Christian educator living in Kansas City, Missouri, where he taught at Midwestern Baptist Theological Seminary for many years. Before that he was minister of education at Crescent Hill Baptist Church, Louisville, Kentucky. "Let the children come" (75) was written in 1983 and is placed with "A Litany for the Dedication of a Child" (76), published in Dr. Sparkman's book *The Salvation and Nurture of the Child: The Story of Emma* (Judson Press, 1983). "Together now the bread we break" (53) is a hymn on the Lord's Supper.

Anne Steele (1716-1788) was the daughter of a timber merchant who served without salary as pastor of the Baptist Church at Broughton, in Hampshire, England. Writing under the *nom de plume* Theodosia with the indication "T" often as the only designation of authorship, Steele published over 150 hymns and metrical psalms during her life. John Julian offers the following critique of her hymns in his famous *Dictionary of Hymnology* (1892): "Although few of them can be placed in the first rank of lyrical compositions, they are almost uniformly simple in language, natural and pleasant in imagery, and full of genuine Christian feeling." It was rare for a woman hymn writer in the eighteenth-century to be as published and sung as much as Anne Steele. She is the author of "The Savior calls, let every ear" (61) and "Father of mercies" [changed to "O God of mercies" for this hymnal] (51), both written in 1760.

Andreas Sudarsono (b. 1949) was born in Central Java, Indonesia, and now works as an editor at the Indonesian Baptist Publishing House in Bandung, West Java. He wrote the hymn "Hanya PadaMu, Tuhan" in his language of Bahasa Indonesia in 1977, and William McElrath provided the English translation, "Only you, O Lord my God" (25). The text is found in the Indonesian hymnal *Nyanyian Pujian* (c. 1981). Basing it on Acts 4:12, Sudarsono wrote this hymn as an expression of grief upon learning of his father's death in 1977. In a letter to the editor, translator William McElrath states, "Thinking that such a text needed a melody with a rather wistful sound, he turned not to his own ancestral Javanese musical forms but to traditional tunes of the Sudanese among whom he was living. Adapting the Sudanese five-tone scale, he wrote a new melody that still sounded distinctly Sudanese and that seemed to fit with the somber mood of his hymn text." Later the hymn was entered in a hymn contest sponsored by *The Baptist Voice*, the Indonesian Baptist news magazine. It was not only the winning hymn, but has been used by non-Baptist groups, including Roman Catholics. McElrath further states, the "widespread use of his Sudanese-sounding hymn coincided with growing international concern for the 33 million Sudanese, widely regarded as the largest unreached ethnic group in the world."

Joan R. Sutton (b. 1930) was born in Louisville, Kentucky, but was raised in Brazil as the daughter of Southern Baptist missionaries. She graduated from Baylor University with a B.A. in English literature and music theory and a B.M. in violin pedagogy. After receiving a Master of Sacred Music degree from Southern Baptist Theological Seminary, she and her husband, Boyd, were appointed as Southern Baptist missionaries to Brazil in 1959. Most of her service was at the South Brazil Seminary (1960-1982), where she taught in most areas of the music program. The Suttons have recently retired and live in Hendersonville, North Carolina. A hymn writer in her own right, she was the general editor of the current hymnal for Brazilian Baptists, *Hinário Para o Culto Cristão*, in 1991. Known as an excellent translator, she also has contributed, among many others, the only complete Portuguese versions of *Messiah* and *Elijah*. Ms. Sutton translated "In these dark, uncertain moments" (26) in 1994 for this hymnal. It is a singing version of the Portuguese text "Nestes tempos de incerteza" written in 1987 by João Fernandes da Silva Neto.

George W. Truett (1867-1944) was pastor of the First Baptist Church, Dallas, Texas, from 1897 until his death in 1944. He also served as president of the Southern Baptist Convention for two years and president of the Baptist World Alliance for five years. The "Litany for Religious Liberty" (34) is adapted from his famous address delivered from the east steps of the national Capitol, May 16, 1920.

Reid S. Trulson (b. 1946) has served American Baptist churches in California and Wisconsin and is currently pastor of the Underwood Memorial Baptist Church in Wauwatosa, Wisconsin. Since receiving two degrees from Fuller Theological Seminary, he has worked as a missionary in Scotland and Ghana and has represented American Baptists in church consultations in the former Soviet Union and South Africa. Trulson is an active member of the Wisconsin Baptist Peace Fellowship and is past president of the American Baptist Board of International Ministries. He contributes the "Litany in Celebration of Religious Liberty" (36).

Davita Joyce Vaughn (b. 1958) graduated from Donnelly College in Kansas City, Missouri, and serves as minister of music at the Evangelistic Center in Kansas City, where her husband, Rev. Arnold Vaughn, is pastor. She wrote "Consecrate me" (64) with Joyce Marie Davis.

Wendell Phillips Whalum (1932-1987) graduated from Booker T. Washington High School in Memphis, Morehouse College in Atlanta, Columbia University, and the University of Iowa. He joined the faculty of Morehouse College in 1953 where he directed the Morehouse College Glee Club and was chair of the music department. Dr. Whalum achieved international recognition as a teacher, organist, conductor, musicologist, arranger, composer, author and lecturer. He made many contributions to the Atlanta community including music positions at Providence Baptist Church, Allen Temple A.M.E. Church, Ebenezer Baptist Church, and Friendship Baptist Church where he was serving when he died. Noted for his musical arrangements of African-American Spirituals, his version of "Guide my feet" (82) is been included in this volume.

Brian A. Wren (b. 1936) is one of the few non-Baptist authors represented in this hymnal. Born in Romford, Essex, England, he studied French at New College, Oxford University, and theology at Mansfield College. Rev. Wren is one of the most published authors of hymn texts in the last half of the twentieth century. With four collections of hymn texts published, he is often sought as a leader of workshops. He now resides in Maine. He contributes three hymns that fill specific topical needs: "Deep in the shadows of the past" (50), a hymn on the formation of scripture; "Give thanks for music-making art" (15), a hymn in celebration of the congregation's song; and "In water we grow" (56), a baptismal hymn that bears a reference to three Southern Baptists in the appendix to the original publication of the text, "To Paul Duke, Stephen Shoemaker, Nancy Foil, and all who stand with them."

Anna York (b. 1945) lives in Chicago where she and her family are members of Cornell Baptist Church, a small church located on the boundary of prosperous, multi-cultural Hyde Park and the ghetto. She serves her church as prayer coordinator and a small group leader. "We now disclaim the power of death" (48) was written as a "Prayer for the cities, composed after the 1992 Los Angeles riots." In a letter to the editor she explains, "When L.A. exploded in riots, our own community was affected. My children were harassed and had stones thrown at them. Some of their friends were robbed and shoved around. The streets were dangerous. I was attacked and robbed between the security doors of our building. The plight of the inner city is very real to us." She has chosen the strong, familiar tune EIN' FESTE BURG both in defiance of the evil that brings cities to the brink of chaos and in the fervent hope that the power of Christ's love will "cause us to love each other."

Philip M. Young (b. 1937) has been minister of music of First Baptist Church, Henderson, North Carolina, since 1959. Born in Greenville, South Carolina, he graduated from North Greenville College and Furman University. Young was honored by Campbell University in 1987 with the Doctor of Humane Letters. He is a prolific composer and hymn writer with over 70 published anthems and cantatas, handbell compositions, hymns and/or hymn tunes. "We stand united in the truth" (44) was written for the Southern Baptist Historical Society meeting in 1986. "Evergreen and ever-fragrant" (37) was written to celebrate the symbolism of the Chrismon trees that are now in many churches during the Advent and Christmas seasons. It is especially appropriate to sing during the Hanging of the Greens.

Mary Zimmer (b. 1947) holds M.Ed., M.S.W., and M.A.C.E. degrees and is the current president of Southern Baptist Women in Ministry. She is the Assistant to the Dean of Christian Education at Southern Baptist Theological Seminary in Louisville, Kentucky. Ms. Zimmer is the author of *Sister Images: Guided Meditations from the Stories of Biblical Women* (Abingdon Press, 1993). She leads retreats and workshops on prayer, biblical women, and women's spirituality. Her "Benediction for Brothers and Sisters Gathered Together" (67) appears in this volume. It is dedicated to the Alliance of Baptists.

INDEX OF TUNE NAMES AND METERS

Tune names in *italics* are suggested as alternate tunes.

INDEX OF COMPOSERS, ARRANGERS, AUTHORS AND TRANSLATORS, AND SOURCES FOR HYMNS, LITANIES AND PRAYERS

An asterisk (*) indicates that further information is available in the Biographical Information on Contributors.

INDEX OF SCRIPTURAL REFERENCES

INDEX OF TOPICS

Selections in *italics* refer to items (prayers or litanies) without music.

INDEX OF TITLES OF HYMNS, LITANIES AND PRAYERS

**Titles of hymns other than first lines are in *italics*.
An asterisk (*) following the title indicates a litany or prayer.**